The Apostles' Creed

TOGETHER WE BELIEVE

MATT CHANDLER

Bible study written by
JEREMY MAXFIELD

LifeWay Press®
Nashville, Tennessee

Published by LifeWay Press® • © 2017 The Village Church
Reprinted October 2017

No part of this book may be reproduced or transmitted in any form or by any
means, electronic or mechanical, including photocopying and recording, or by any
information storage or retrieval system, except as may be expressly permitted in
writing by the publisher. Requests for permission should be addressed in writing
to LifeWay Press®; One LifeWay Plaza; Nashville, TN 37234-0152.

ISBN 978-1-4300-5457-3 • Item 006103003

Dewey decimal classification: 238
Subject headings: APOSTLES' CREED / GOSPEL / DOCTRINAL THEOLOGY

Unless otherwise indicated, Scripture quotations are from the ESV® Bible (The
Holy Bible, English Standard Version®), copyright © 2001 by Crossway, a pub-
lishing ministry of Good News Publishers. Used by permission. All rights reserved.
Scripture quotations marked NKJV are taken from the New King James Version®.
Copyright © 1982 by Thomas Nelson. Used by permission. All rights reserved.

To order additional copies of this resource, write to LifeWay Resources Customer
Service; One LifeWay Plaza; Nashville, TN 37234-0113; fax 615-251-5933; phone
toll free 800-458-2772; order online at LifeWay.com; email orderentry@lifeway.
com; or visit the LifeWay Christian Store serving you.

Printed in the United States of America

Groups Ministry Publishing • LifeWay Resources
One LifeWay Plaza • Nashville, TN 37234-0152

Contents

Week 1

Week 2

Week 3

Week 4

Week 5

Week 6

Week 7

Week 8

Week 9

Week 10

Week 11

Week 12

I believe in God the Father Almighty,
    Creator of heaven and earth,
And in Jesus Christ, His only Son, our Lord,
Who was conceived by the Holy Spirit;
    born of the virgin Mary;
Suffered under Pontius Pilate;
    was crucified, dead, and buried.
He descended to hell; the third day
    He rose again from the dead;
He ascended to heaven and sits on the
    right hand of the Father Almighty,
From whence He shall come to
    judge the living and the dead.
I believe in the Holy Spirit,
The holy catholic church,
    the communion of saints,
The forgiveness of sins,
The resurrection of the body,
    and the life everlasting. Amen.

Introduction

It's easy for our culture of individuality and innovation to shape the way we think about the church. So what should we believe? Should Christians try to be more accepting of a postmodern worldview? With so many questions, opinions, and interpretations among people today—even within the church—what should we all agree on as essential to Christian faith?

Finding its genesis in the apostles' teachings, the Apostles' Creed contains essential Christian doctrines and beliefs that summarize the gospel and make up the foundation of our faith. The scriptural truths contained in the creed help us operate from good theology, with the knowledge that our faith is rooted in truth and a rich history that spans past, present, and future. The lines of the creed aren't mere words. They convey the essence of what we confess and believe as the body of Christ.

About the Author

MATT CHANDLER serves as the lead pastor of teaching at The Village Church in the Dallas/Fort Worth metroplex. He came to The Village in December 2002 and describes his tenure as a replanting effort to change the theological and philosophical culture of the congregation. The church has witnessed a tremendous response, growing from 160 people to more than 11,000, including campuses in Flower Mound, Dallas, Plano, and Fort Worth.

Alongside his current role as lead pastor, Matt is involved in church-planting efforts both locally and internationally through The Village, as well as in various strategic partnerships. Prior to accepting the pastorate at The Village, Matt had a vibrant itinerant ministry for more than 10 years that gave him the opportunity to speak to thousands of people in America and abroad about the glory of God and the beauty of Jesus.

Matt is the author of *To Live Is Christ, to Die Is Gain; Mingling of Souls;* and *The Explicit Gospel Bible Study* (LifeWay, 2012). He's also a coauthor of *Creature of the Word* (LifeWay, 2012).

Other than knowing Jesus, Matt's greatest joy is being married to Lauren and being the dad to their three children: Audrey, Reid, and Norah.

How to Use This Study

The Apostles' Creed provides a guided process for individuals and small groups to explore 12 core tenets of Christianity. This Bible study book includes 12 weeks of content, each divided into three main sections: "Group Study," "Family Discipleship," and "Personal Study." A leader guide is also provided to prepare those who are leading groups through this journey.

GROUP STUDY

Regardless of the day of the week your group meets, each week of content begins with a group session. This group session is designed to last 90 minutes, with approximately 45 minutes dedicated to video teaching and another 45 minutes to group discussion. Meeting even longer than 90 minutes will allow more time for participants to interact with one another.

Each group study uses the following format to facilitate simple yet meaningful interaction among group members, with God's Word, and with the video teaching.

START

This section includes questions to get the conversation started, a review of the previous week's study to reinforce the content, and an introduction to the new content for the current week.

WATCH

This page includes key points from the video teaching, along with space for taking notes as participants watch the video.

DISCUSS

This page includes discussion questions that guide the group to respond to the video teaching and to relevant Bible passages.

FAMILY DISCIPLESHIP

The Apostles' Creed presents a great opportunity for families to consider the truths of the gospel together. The "Family Discipleship" section provides discussion, activities, and memorization opportunities that encourage families to engage with this material on a deeper level.

ENGAGE

This page will guide your family to consider the truths of the gospel by utilizing the following framework: "Time," "Moments," and "Milestones." Use this framework for family discipleship in your home and on the go.

MEMORIZE

Space is provided for participants who want to memorize the Apostles' Creed as a family. Use this page to write from memory the sections of the creed you've covered up to that point in the study.

PERSONAL STUDY

Three personal studies are provided each week to take individuals deeper into Scripture and to supplement the content introduced in the group study. With biblical teaching and interactive questions, these sections challenge individuals to grow in their understanding of God's Word and to make practical application to their lives.

LEADER GUIDE

On pages 154–59 at the back of this book you'll find a leader guide that will help you prepare each week. Use this guide to gain a broad understanding of the content for each week and to learn ways you can engage members at different levels of life-changing discussion.

The Apostles' Creed Grid

Throughout this study we'll examine and apply the doctrines outlined in the Apostles' Creed by using a four-part grid as a filter to draw out key truths. The personal study in week 2 will introduce the grid, and the personal study in weeks 3–12 will explore a specific phrase in the creed by examining it through each of the four areas of focus and application.

SYMMETRY: *The creed helps us develop better symmetry as Christians, giving us a more robust understanding of biblical teaching.*

As Christians, it's easy to stick with what we already know. Either we don't grow and remain immature with a minimal, two-dimensional faith, or even if we're growing, we become out of balance instead of developing a holistic, well-rounded faith. The creed helps us intentionally cover the doctrinal spectrum. Think of it like an exercise routine. Just as you don't need to work the same muscle group every day, neglecting the others, you need to broaden your understanding of the full scope of biblical truth. Believing Jesus is your Savior is vital, but it's also necessary to recognize that He's called you into a relationship with the church. A Christian who settles for believing in Jesus as Savior but never develops a love for the church is out of balance and ultimately unhealthy. We desire symmetry or balance to be well rounded in our doctrinal understanding as mature disciples.

CLARITY: *The creed helps us with clarity, making clear who God is.*

While symmetry applies to our overall knowledge of core biblical doctrines, clarity is a more specific focus on what we believe about God and the world. By and large, American evangelicals seem to be terribly confused about who God is, what He's up to, what He's like, and what He's about. Surveys reveal shocking misconceptions, many of which are similar to the heresies that the Apostles' Creed was intended to refute. For example, is the Holy Spirit a He or an It? Is Jesus both fully God and fully man? Did Jesus literally die? Did He have a physical body when resurrected? The Christian life isn't about our preferences or opinions or the latest cultural trends; it's about God. What you believe about God is the most important thing in your life; it shapes all your attitudes and actions.

COMMUNITY: *The creed informs our community, whom we belong to, and whom we're with.*

As Christians who believe the doctrines summarized in the Apostles' Creed, we're part of a people who have been around for thousands of years. We're part of a people who go back to the beginning of humankind, when God called first people to Himself. Throughout history God's people, those He has chosen and called to Himself, have thrived and worshiped the one true God. We're part of that tradition. We're a global people. People all over the earth will gather this weekend because they share the beliefs expressed in the creed. They'll rejoice in it, they'll be shaped by it, and massive numbers of them will recite the creed together. We've been woven into something much bigger than us. The fabric created by God makes us stronger than any of us can ever be on our own. It's diverse, it's beautiful, and it's global.

As Christianity in the United States, having enjoyed great favor the past 150 years, now starts to fall out of favor, any effort to define ourselves by secondary beliefs must also fade away. The creed shows us what's primary in the Christian faith. We're a creedal people, united by truth that supersedes any other differences in our culture and sets us apart as a distinct community of faith.

COUNSEL: *The creed informs the way we counsel ourselves and others.*

Counsel is essentially the point of application. How do symmetry, clarity, and community lead to a change in your perspective? How do you think and act differently? What do you tell yourself or others as a result of believing the doctrines in the creed? For example, if you believe Christ will return to judge the living and dead, that will affect the way you think about sin and the way you warn and encourage others in regard to personal holiness. Think of the ammunition that belief provides against sin. When you grow in your understanding of the person of God, the work of Christ, and the power of the Holy Spirit, you'll think differently.

The four parts of this grid work together to form a cohesive framework to help us grow within the long tradition of orthodox Christian beliefs. Symmetry in our understanding of the Bible leads to more clarity about who God is. The better we understand God and the big picture of the Bible, the better we can counsel ourselves and one another in the community of faith. As we counsel one another in community, we grow in symmetry and clarity. The result should be an ever-deepening maturity and a closer walk of obedience with our Lord Jesus Christ.

Week One

I believe in God the Father Almighty,
    Creator of heaven and earth,
And in Jesus Christ, His only Son, our Lord,
Who was conceived by the Holy Spirit;
    born of the virgin Mary;
Suffered under Pontius Pilate;
    was crucified, dead, and buried.
He descended to hell; the third day
    He rose again from the dead;
He ascended to heaven and sits on the
    right hand of the Father Almighty,
From whence He shall come to judge
    the living and the dead.
I believe in the Holy Spirit,
The holy catholic church,
    the communion of saints,
The forgiveness of sins,
The resurrection of the body,
    and the life everlasting. Amen.

Group Study

START

I BELIEVE IN

Welcome everyone to week 1 of The Apostles' Creed.
Use this page to begin the group session.

Let's begin by taking a few minutes to get to know one another.

Ask members of the group to introduce themselves by sharing their names, members of their immediate families, and where they grew up.

What was your favorite school song, team cheer, or student tradition?

Things like school songs, cheers, and traditions unite us with other like-minded people in the present and in the past. Gathering together and raising our voices in a unified declaration create a powerful sense of confidence, pride, and identity. Each of us desires to belong to something greater than ourselves. Even in today's society, which celebrates individuality and innovation, there's still nothing that compares to the energy, commitment, and reverence generated by a united community, group celebration, and proud tradition.

It's easy for our cultural values of individuality and innovation to undermine the unity that God intended for His church. For the next 12 weeks we'll consider the value of declaring our shared beliefs with one another and with the long line of Christians who came before us.

*Read the Apostles' Creed aloud as a group
before watching video session 1.*

WATCH

Use this viewer guide to follow along and take notes as you watch video session 1.

THE APOSTLES' CREED WILL HELP US WITH:

1. Symmetry—a robust understanding of the God of the Bible
2. Clarity—who God is
3. Community—whom we belong to and whom we are with
4. Counsel—to ourselves and to others

Creeds do not hold any authority in and of themselves, but rather, they point outside themselves to the ultimate authority of the Word of God.

THE APOSTLES' CREED HAS BEEN USED:

- to correct error;
- as a tool in the spiritual formation of God's people.

Believing leads to action, and knowing may or may not.

Belief is birthed in the heart.

The message of the Christian faith isn't that we have done anything, but rather, we have believed that Someone has.

We aren't chained to rote religious activity, but we have a Savior who has accomplished all that we desire for us.

The Apostles' Creed shows us what's primary.

When the early church recited this, it was simultaneously their greatest act of rebellion and their greatest act of allegiance.

This beautiful moment when the people of God recited this creed, they said, "We don't believe the story that our culture is telling."

DISCUSS

Discuss the video segment, using the following questions.

Before we watched the video, we read the Apostles' Creed as a group. What's the significance of reciting the Apostles' Creed together? Why is it significant that the first word of the creed is *I*?

Why is it important for Christians to articulate and agree on what we believe?

Why did Matt distinguish between the authority of Scripture and of a creed?

READ ROMANS 10:9-10.

How do belief and action relate to salvation, as described in these verses? What distinction did Matt make between knowing and believing?

In what specific ways do our historical Christian beliefs, as outlined in the Apostles' Creed, rebel against our present-day culture?

How does a Christian experience freedom in believing the gospel?

Because the Apostles' Creed is a faithful, truthful summary of Christian doctrine as revealed in the Bible, notice that no article of the creed can be removed without detracting from the gospel. Every point is essential.

Why is it important to preserve the full teaching of the gospel, not just the parts that are easier to believe?

What's your primary observation about the teaching on belief?

What remaining thoughts or questions do you have?

Encourage members to complete the following personal studies before the next group session.

Family Discipleship

ENGAGE

The Apostles' Creed presents a great opportunity for families to consider the truths of the gospel together by utilizing the following framework for family discipleship: time, moments, and milestones.

☐ **TIME. Begin memorizing the Apostles' Creed as a family. This week should be fairly easy: "I believe." Explain what a creed is and the importance of knowing what we believe about God and why.**

☐ **MOMENTS. Look for opportunities to identify other belief systems or worldviews your family encounters. Point out that everything people do originates from their belief systems. How does the way we live point to our belief in God?**

☐ **MILESTONES. How will your family celebrate the occasions when your kids come to know the Lord? When your kids are baptized, what are some ways you could share with your unbelieving family and friends what God has done? Commemorate your own baptism by sharing your testimony with your family on the anniversary of your baptism.**

MEMORIZE

*Use this page to practice writing
the Apostles' Creed from memory.*

Personal Study

DAY 1

The Apostles' Creed begins with the words "I believe in." When you recite the creed in your group each week, you're declaring to the world that you believe the Christian story is both good and true. God the Father is reconciling the world to Himself in the Person and work of Jesus Christ, through the power of the Holy Spirit.

The creed is more than just an individual statement; it's both personal and corporate. You're "surrounded by so great a cloud of witnesses" (Heb. 12:1), and when you recite the creed, you publicly identify with the church—a group of people who believe in the work of the triune God.

In the early church, uttering the word *credo* ("I believe") meant identifying in the closest possible way with the gospel. Often new believers recited the Apostles' Creed during their baptismal ceremonies and were then welcomed into the fellowship of the saints. When believers said the creed, they were identifying themselves as citizens of a different kingdom—the kingdom of God. This meant, and still means today, that believers could face persecution, alienation, and even death. The creed is far more than a list of propositions; it's the summary of the apostolic faith that has been practiced throughout church history.

READ HEBREWS 11:1-2.

The beauty and tension of these Scripture verses come from the fact that based on what has happened in the past, Christians have assurance and conviction in placing their hope and belief in something they've never seen.

Though we believe in the existence of God since before time began and in His work that began human history with the creation of the world, a man named Abram was the first in a long tradition of people who put their belief in God.

READ GENESIS 12:1-4.

We learn more about Abram, later called Abraham, throughout the pages of Scripture in a beautiful account of a vibrant belief in action. His story is central in the historical record of faith that unfolds in Hebrews 11.

Why do you think details about Abram's age, family, and land were included in Genesis 12:1-4? What do they reveal about belief?

What experiences have challenged you to consider how seriously you believe something about God and/or His Word? How did those moments shape your perspective on life and what it means to live by faith?

Abram's belief in God affected his own life, the lives of his family members, and the lives of people around him. The same is true today. Your beliefs have been shaped by other people; your faith is a testimony that affects the people around you as well.

Identify specific people in your life who have been examples of living by faith. How did their actions shape your understanding of the Christian life?

Humans are made for community, and that's why the creed is confessed together by the entire believing community. However, even when a local congregation recites the creed in unison, the first word of each statement of the creed is *I*. Popular culture asserts that all people should have the opportunity, even the right, to define themselves. The Apostles' Creed reminds us that the truth isn't up for redefinition.

Prayer

Grant me faith, Father in heaven. Give me a faith that's focused on Your work, the work of Your Son, and the work of the Holy Spirit throughout the history of the world. Even when I struggle to believe, sustain me by Your grace. Help me walk by faith, not by sight, and grow in my affection toward You as I learn more about Your mighty deeds. Help me not to depart from this apostolic faith You've given to all believers by Your providential and glorious mercy. Amen.

DAY 2

Whether or not people go to church and whether or not they know what the verse says, it's hard to go through life without seeing a reference to John 3:16.

Use this space to write John 3:16 from memory. If you don't have the verse memorized, look it up in your Bible and copy it here.

How would you explain the importance of belief, according to John 3:16?

Describe the moment when you first believed in Jesus. If you haven't had a moment like this in your life, record the name of your group leader and/or a trusted Christian friend whom you'll commit to ask questions about personal belief in Jesus.

This popular verse is part of a conversation Jesus had with a Jewish leader named Nicodemus (see John 3:1-21). Jesus' words boldly declared what it truly meant to believe in God. In that culture the majority of God's covenant people had grown to believe that their relationship and right standing before God were based on two things: observing Jewish religious traditions and being born into Jewish families. However, Jesus said anyone could have a relationship with God—if they truly believed in His Son for salvation.

A similar trap of mistaken belief in what makes people right with God exists today. If someone grew up in a Christian home or is a morally good person, it's easy to believe he or she is a Christian. The Bible is crystal clear, though, that merely believing correct things about God won't get anybody into heaven.

This point can't be overstated: cultural Christianity won't save you.

In which area(s) do you find yourself inclined to measure your relationship with God?

- ☐ **Having a good family**
- ☐ **Living a moral life**
- ☐ **Going to church**
- ☐ **Studying the Bible**
- ☐ **Volunteering to serve**
- ☐ **Giving money to a ministry**
- ☐ **Being recognized as a leader**

What's the danger of basing the certainty of your salvation on external behaviors like the previous ones?

Pisteuō, the Greek word translated as *believes* in John 3:16, has a richer meaning than the simple understanding of facts. To believe in something means to commit and to give your trust. Of course, trust and commitment find expressions in external behavior, so belief isn't just a matter of head knowledge. It's a matter of the heart's devotion.

It's easy for John 3:16 to become so familiar that the gravity of the situation is lost. Don't let words like *love, life,* and *saved* distract you from *perish* and *condemned.* You need to wrestle with each of those realities until you come to grips with what's at stake here. Christian belief is infinitely more than an adherence to a moral code or a knowledge of religious facts. True belief—life-changing commitment and trust—is a matter of eternal life or death.

Prayer

Spend time reflecting on the fact that your relationship with God isn't based on who you are, where you were born, or what you know. Thank Him that you can live eternally as part of His family by truly believing in His only Son, Jesus. Commit yourself to trust Christ wholeheartedly.

DAY 3

Unlike Matthew and Luke, John didn't begin his Gospel account by providing a detailed record of Jesus' birth. Instead, the Book of John begins with a beautiful description of the divine personhood and redemptive purpose of Jesus' incarnation.

READ JOHN 1:11-13.

What's the result of belief in Christ, according to these verses?

From the very beginning of the book, John told his readers that Jesus came to change their lives forever if they believed in Him. The opening words revealed that through faith in Jesus, anyone could become a child of God. However, the people who should have recognized and believed in Jesus—the Jews—didn't receive Him.

The account of Nicodemus in John 3 illustrates the lack of understanding among God's people. Nicodemus was a religious expert who couldn't wrap his mind around the truth of salvation by faith in the Son of God. This Jewish leader couldn't understand how "whoever believes in" Jesus (v. 16) could be born again into God's eternal family.

The closing chapters of the Book of John lead us to an unmistakable conclusion about what it means to believe in Jesus.

READ JOHN 20:24-31.

Notice that Jesus didn't leave Thomas in a state of confusion and doubt. Jesus met this disciple in the midst of his struggle to believe. Thomas had been a devoted follower of Jesus. He had committed to literally follow Jesus every day for almost three years. He had put his trust in Jesus. But after the crucifixion Thomas didn't know what was true.

Put yourself in his position. It would have been difficult to trust your own judgment and hopes after such an unexpected traumatic experience. Everything you thought you knew seemed to have been wrong. Of course, you would have wanted to believe Jesus had been raised from the dead. But if it was true, why would you be the only person without the same experience as the other disciples?

What have you struggled to believe about the Christian faith?

How did you come to a point of belief, even if you still don't understand?

In what ways is it comforting to read that even one of Jesus' disciples struggled with whether he could believe what he was being told about Jesus?

What objections do people have about the validity of Christianity?

Whom do you know who has doubts about the Christian faith?

How can you help share the truth about your Lord and your God, the resurrected Jesus?

The Gospel of John comes full circle in the final words of the book. John clearly restated in unmistakable terms his desire for the church. As a believer, you're a part of this legacy.

Prayer

Thank God that in His grace He has come to you, speaking
your name, so that you can believe in His Son, Jesus Christ.
Take time to worship Him now as your personal Lord and Savior.

Week Two

I believe in God the Father Almighty,
    Creator of heaven and earth,
And in Jesus Christ, His only Son, our Lord,
Who was conceived by the Holy Spirit;
    born of the virgin Mary;
Suffered under Pontius Pilate;
    was crucified, dead, and buried.
He descended to hell; the third day
    He rose again from the dead;
He ascended to heaven and sits on the
    right hand of the Father Almighty,
From whence He shall come to judge
    the living and the dead.
I believe in the Holy Spirit,
The holy catholic church,
    the communion of saints,
The forgiveness of sins,
The resurrection of the body,
    and the life everlasting. Amen.

Group Study

START

GOD THE FATHER ALMIGHTY, CREATOR OF HEAVEN AND EARTH

Welcome everyone to week 2 of The Apostles' Creed.
Use this page to begin the group session.

Let's begin by taking a few minutes to review last week's study.

What was the most meaningful or challenging part of your personal study or family discipleship from "I believe in"? What did you learn or experience in a specific way this week?

Day 2 of last week's personal study included a checklist of things other than faith with which we may be tempted to measure our Christian identities and relationships with God. Which did you select and why?

Last week we established the importance of belief. From this point on, we'll focus each week on specific doctrines that make up the core of our Christian faith. This week we'll begin our study where the Bible begins: "God the Father Almighty, Creator of heaven and earth."

Read the Apostles' Creed aloud as a group before watching video session 2.

WATCH

*Use this viewer guide to follow along and
take notes as you watch video session 2.*

Our God is an infinitely powerful and yet intensely personal Father.

Only the Christian God in the ancient Near East was One who loved His people
and sought their good.

It is only a selfish, unloving father that always says yes.

Our daily bread is not that God gives you everything you want. It's that He gives
you what you actually need.

The gospel not only reconciles us to the Father but then begins to reconcile us
to one another.

1. SYMMETRY
The Bible is vocal and loud about God's delight in you, His pleasure in you,
and His desire to commune with you.

2. CLARITY
To be a God of love is to have wrath.

If God loves you, He will expose your secret sin.

3. COMMUNITY
We walk together as the communion of saints brought together by this Father.

4. COUNSEL
If God the Father Almighty is infinitely powerful and intensely personal,
that should shape how we counsel ourselves and others.

DISCUSS

Discuss the video segment, using the following questions.

Matt said we all have to wrestle with the question of whether we believe God is good. Why is that question foundational?

When have you struggled to believe God is good? When have you wanted something and didn't understand why God wasn't saying yes?

How does it affect your view of God to know that He delights in you? How does it affect your view of yourself?

How often do you think of God as Almighty Creator? How should this title of God shape our understanding of Him?

Why do love and wrath necessarily go together in God's character? Why would a loving God expose secret sin?

What are the relational implications of being united with other Christians by a powerful yet personal Father?

Which of the two attributes do you tend to think of most when you think about God: powerful or personal? Why do you relate to Him in that way? Why is it vital to relate to God as both/and, not either/or?

READ MATTHEW 6:9-13.

How does each phrase in the Model Prayer reveal God's character as personal yet powerful?

What's your primary observation about the teaching on "God the Father Almighty, Creator of heaven and earth"?

What remaining thoughts or questions do you have?

Encourage members to complete the following personal studies before the next group session.

Family Discipleship

ENGAGE

The Apostles' Creed presents a great opportunity for families to consider the truths of the gospel together by utilizing the following framework for family discipleship: time, moments, and milestones.

- ☐ **TIME. Continue to memorize the Apostles' Creed as a family by adding this week's article to what you memorized last week. By the end of the Bible study, you will have memorized the entire creed.**

- ☐ **MOMENTS. Look for opportunities to point out what God has created—people and nature. How do you see God's design in creation as a good gift from a good Father?**

- ☐ **MILESTONES. Consider the way your family celebrates Father's Day. What can you do that points both to the fatherly nature of God and to God the Father who helps you? Encourage and pray for the sanctification of our earthly fathers.**

MEMORIZE

*Use this page to practice writing
the Apostles' Creed from memory.*

DAY 1

Have you ever been in darkness so complete that you literally couldn't see your hand in front of your face? No amount of time can allow your eyes to adjust when you're in total darkness. Now imagine a full moon on a dark night. It allows you to see the world around you in a way that would otherwise be impossible. Now imagine being in that same spot in the middle of a sunny day. You have a clear, more complete picture.

The Apostles' Creed is like the moon. It's not the source of light. As the moon reflects the light of the sun, the creed merely reflects the truth of Scripture. God's Word is the sun—our source of truth. Remember that you aren't studying the creed. It's a summary of what we believe. You're studying the Bible. It's the totality of what we believe. The creed should point you to the truth revealed in God's Word.

The creed starts where the Bible starts: with God.

READ GENESIS 1:1.

The Bible begins with one of the most stunning, reality-shaping phrases possible.

What's the first thing we learn about God from this verse? Why is this an important starting point for the entire Bible?

God created from nothing. He didn't simply fashion preexisting creation into new shapes and forms; He brought creation into being by His word (see Gen. 1; Heb. 11:3). By the incomparable power of His will, God spoke everything into existence. He's Almighty.

READ PSALM 8.

Where do you see God's power and creativity on display in the world today? What's particularly awe-inspiring in God's creation?

How does believing that God created you as uniquely valuable shape your perspective in life and your posture before God?

As the Apostles' Creed states, God the Father Almighty is the "Creator of heaven and earth." Referring to Christ, theologian Abraham Kuyper said, "There is not a square inch in the whole domain of our human existence over which Christ, who is Sovereign over *all,* does not cry: 'Mine!' "[1] These words beautifully capture the fact that every bit of every created thing rightly belongs to God.

Why is it important to believe the fact that God is all-powerful and has authority over all things?

What in your life do you practically and functionally deny as belonging to God and therefore refuse to recognize is under His authority?

What actions will you take to acknowledge that everything belongs to God?

Prayer

Father, by Your mighty word You've brought all things into existence.
I can rightly call You my Maker and Creator. Everything belongs to You,
my Father. Continually give me eyes to see Your beauty and ears to
hear Your marvelous truth. Thank You that not only are You my Creator,
but You're also my Father. Draw me ever closer into fellowship with
You, through the work of Your Son and by Your Holy Spirit. Amen.

1. Abraham Kuyper, as quoted in *Abraham Kuyper: A Centennial Reader,*
   ed. James D. Bratt (Grand Rapids, MI: Eerdmans, 1998), 461.

DAY 2

Although God is the almighty, transcendent Creator of all things, He isn't a generic deity. The God of the Bible has given Himself to us as Trinity. We believe God has eternally existed as one essence and three distinct Persons: God the Father, God the Son, and God the Holy Spirit. Each Person is fully God, yet at the same time, there's only one God. Specifically, this part of the creed addresses the first Person of the Godhead: God the Father.

The first line of the Apostles' Creed confesses that we believe in God the Father. This line clearly indicates that we don't believe in a God who's far off and distant but in a God who's infinitely powerful yet intensely personal.

List as many characteristics as you can that describe a good father.

READ EPHESIANS 1:3-14.

In what ways does God act like a father to us, His children? List the different descriptions of God in this passage and identify what He has done for His children.

Why is it important to believe that God had a plan for your life since the beginning of time?

How should it affect the way you live today, as you face different decisions, circumstances, and relationships, to know that God has a plan for the future?

Consider the meaning of an inheritance through earthly relationships. How does this concept apply to our relationship with God? What's the inheritance for people whom God has adopted as His children?

Have you wrestled with any obstacles to trusting that the Father's care for you is best? If so, what are they?

How has God the Father shown faithfulness and love to you?

With whom can you share what you've experienced to be true about a relationship with God through faith in Christ?

Prayer

Thank God for His generous, sacrificial love for you, expressed in the giving of His Son, Jesus, and of His Holy Spirit. Confess any areas of your life in which you aren't trusting His will and glorifying His name as your good Father. Ask God for wisdom to recognize opportunities to share the good news of salvation from sin, adoption through faith in Christ, and the hope of eternal life as a coheir in the family of God.

DAY 3

Because every believer enjoys a personal relationship with God, the creed reminds us that we're also in fellowship with the millions of Christians around the world and from every age who believe these affirmations to be true about God.

Our belief in God is more than a theological point of agreement about correct doctrine. A right understanding of God is foundational to the way we live the Christian life. It has practical implications for our relationships with God and one another. Let's review this week's points of symmetry, clarity, community, and counsel that arise from belief in God.

1. SYMMETRY

As our Creator, God knows what's best for us. He made us. A creator of something knows how it works best, right? God created everything. He created the heavens and the earth and everything in them—including you. Everything has a purpose. The design is intentional, intricate, and beautiful. Throughout the story of creation, the common refrain in Genesis 1 is "It was good." The Bible is vocal and loud about God's delight in you, His pleasure in you, and His desire to commune with you. In other words, He loves you.

How does it affect the way you relate to God when you believe that He created you and wants what's best for you?

2. CLARITY

Because a father is wiser than his children, he wants what's best for them, even if they don't understand or like it at the moment. As part of God's family through belief in His only Son (see John 3:16), we have to take seriously the consequences of rebellion.

Sin is rebellion against the good design of our Creator and the loving desire of our Father. We need to realize that sin destroys us and our relationship with God. Because God knows and wants what's best for us, He hates sin. Because He loves us, He pours out wrath on that which destroys us and our relationships with Him and one another.

READ HEBREWS 12:5-11.

How does viewing God as Father affect the way you view sin? The way you view God's discipline?

3. COMMUNITY

READ GALATIANS 3:26-28 AND 1 JOHN 3.

How should belief in God as a good Creator and a loving Father change the way you view and treat other people? Whom have you not been treating as a brother or a sister, created and loved by God?

4. COUNSEL

By the authority of God's word at creation, we've been made His children. What He says to be true is true. A right belief in God also gives each person in the family of God the responsibility to remind one another of the seriousness of sin. If our Father's love includes wrath toward sin, then we should love members of His family enough to address sin and to welcome correction from others when they confront our sin.

Who will speak truth into your life as a brother or a sister through faith in Christ? Whom do you need to remind of the goodness of God or of the seriousness of sin?

Prayer

Take a few minutes to let the profound reality of 1 John 3:1 sink into your heart. In this one simple statement you can see God as both a powerful Creator and a loving Father. Pray that this truth will reorient your life, giving you a confidence in and conviction of the awesome privilege of being a child of God.

Week Three

I believe in God the Father Almighty,
　　Creator of heaven and earth,
And in Jesus Christ, His only Son, our Lord,
Who was conceived by the Holy Spirit;
　　born of the virgin Mary;
Suffered under Pontius Pilate;
　　was crucified, dead, and buried.
He descended to hell; the third day
　　He rose again from the dead;
He ascended to heaven and sits on the
　　right hand of the Father Almighty,
From whence He shall come to judge
　　the living and the dead.
I believe in the Holy Spirit,
The holy catholic church,
　　the communion of saints,
The forgiveness of sins,
The resurrection of the body,
　　and the life everlasting. Amen.

Group Study

START

AND IN JESUS CHRIST, HIS ONLY SON, OUR LORD

Welcome everyone to week 3 of The Apostles' Creed.
Use this page to begin the group session.

Let's begin by taking a few minutes to review last week's study.

What was the most meaningful or challenging part of your personal study or family discipleship from "God the Father Almighty, Creator of heaven and earth"? What did you learn or experience in a specific way this week?

Day 3 of each week calls for interaction with the grid Matt introduced for understanding and applying the core doctrines summarized in the Apostles' Creed. Which of the four areas were most applicable this week and why? (Refer to pp. 32–33 if needed.)

1. Symmetry: a balanced, robust understanding of biblical teaching
2. Clarity: a picture of who God truly is, not who we want Him to be
3. Community: an understanding of how to relate to one another as Christians
4. Counsel: an ability to speak biblical truth to ourselves and to others

In the Apostles' Creed we see the divine relationship within the triune Godhead. This week we move from "God the Father" to the second Person of the Trinity: "Jesus Christ, His only Son, our Lord."

Read the Apostles' Creed aloud as a group
before watching video session 3.

WATCH

Use this viewer guide to follow along and take notes as you watch video session 3.

Jesus is the King of everything.

JESUS IS UNIQUE IN HIS SONSHIP

    1. He is coeternal with God the Father.

    2. He walks in a distinct authority.

    3. He is a part of the Godhead.

When Jesus is called Lord, He is called the Savior of the world.

1. SYMMETRY

Many of us feel that Jesus can be our Savior with no submission to Him being King, and this is a foreign concept in the Bible.

2. CLARITY

If Jesus is who He says He is, we cannot be indifferent to that claim.

3. COMMUNITY

God Himself comes and makes peace with the rebellious.

The world is broken, and we've got good news.

4. COUNSEL

You have a King who is the Creator of all things. He designed things to work a specific way for your joy and for the glory of God.

There will come a day where Christ returns to judge the living and the dead.

DISCUSS

Discuss the video segment, using the following questions.

How is Jesus equal to God the Father? How is He distinct as the Son?

READ MATTHEW 16:13-16.

How would you describe the difference between knowing what people say about Jesus and personally knowing Jesus? What positive yet incorrect or incomplete ideas do people have about Jesus today?

Why is it important to recognize and confess Jesus as Christ (Savior), God's only Son, and Lord (King)?

Why is it common in our culture to claim Jesus as Savior without submitting to Him as King? Has this unbiblical mentality been a part of your own testimony? If so, what happened to change your perspective?

What did Matt mean when he said, "If Jesus is who He says He is, we cannot be indifferent to that claim." How does that assertion affect your view of evangelism? Discipleship? Personal obedience? What does indifference look like in your life?

If sin can be understood as rebellion against our King, why is the gospel such good news? How does it unite us as Christians?

How does the belief that your Creator and King designed things to work for your joy affect your view of sin? Of submission to Him?

What's your primary observation about the teaching on "And in Jesus Christ, His only Son, our Lord"?

What remaining thoughts or questions do you have?

Encourage members to complete the following personal studies before the next group session.

Family Discipleship

ENGAGE

The Apostles' Creed presents a great opportunity for families to consider the truths of the gospel together by utilizing the following framework for family discipleship: time, moments, and milestones.

- ☐ **TIME. Continue to memorize the Apostles' Creed as a family by adding this week's article, "And in Jesus Christ, His only Son, our Lord," to what you memorized last week. Consider reciting it during a meal or during drive times.**

- ☐ **MOMENTS. As you pray together this week, point out occasions when you conclude prayers with "In Jesus' name." Talk about the meaning of this phrase. Why do Christians pray that way? For clues read John 14:12-14.**

- ☐ **MILESTONES. *Jesus* means "the Lord saves." *Christ* is a title meaning "Messiah" or "Anointed One." Read Matthew 1:18-21. In what ways is the giving or receiving of a name a milestone? Talk to your family about what their names mean or why you gave your children their particular names. What are you saying about them every time you say their names? Then talk about the significance of Jesus' name and its origin.**

MEMORIZE

*Use this page to practice writing
the Apostles' Creed from memory.*

Personal Study

DAY 1

If you attended a function at which Queen Elizabeth was present, she wouldn't be introduced to you as Liz Windsor. She would be presented as "Her Majesty Elizabeth II, by the grace of God, of the United Kingdom of Great Britain and Northern Ireland and of her other realms and territories queen, head of the commonwealth, defender of the faith." Each part of the queen's title explains her true identity. The same can be said of this week's portion of the Apostles' Creed. It presents God's Son to us in terms that communicate who He is and the authority He commands.

When God made the birth of Jesus known to His earthly father, Joseph, two names were given: *Jesus* and *Immanuel* (see Matt. 1:18-25). The Gospel of Matthew explains that *Immanuel* means "God with us" (v. 23). The account reveals that Jesus is the incarnate God. The name *Jesus,* a common name at the time, means "the Lord saves." When we see the name *Jesus,* we're reminded of our Lord as both the Son of God and the historical man who bore that name. Jesus' earthly name points us to the truth of His full humanity.

READ ROMANS 1:1-4.

What evidence do these verses present for Jesus' humanity and divinity?

True belief in Jesus is at the heart of a relationship with God. The most popular verse in the Bible summarizes the gospel of Jesus, including His identity:

> *God so loved the world that He gave His only begotten Son, that whoever believes in Him should not perish but have everlasting life.*
> **JOHN 3:16, NKJV**

Many Christians recognize the phrase "only begotten son" from the King James translation of this verse. *Begotten,* to modern ears, sounds like a synonym for *created*. However, the Greek word from which it's translated is *monogeneses,* expressing not that Jesus was created but that He's uniquely God the Son. Jesus is equal in substance and coeternal with the Father. Jesus has always been God, but there was a moment in time when God the Son was "begotten"; He took on flesh and dwelt with us. Even before the incarnation, the second Person of the Trinity was always—and is eternally—the Son of the Father (see Col. 1:15-20).

READ HEBREWS 1.

Last week you studied some key characteristics of God. In what ways did the writer of Hebrews intentionally describe Jesus as being divine?

READ HEBREWS 2:17-18.

Why is it essential to salvation that Jesus is both fully God and fully man?

READ HEBREWS 4:14-16.

What does this passage say we gain in Jesus' humanity?

The writer of Hebrews used the word *propitiation* to describe the purpose of Jesus' life and death as God and man (see 2:17). Our sin deserves the wrath of God, as we studied last week. In His love for us, God poured out wrath on His Son for our sin but provided grace and mercy through Him as well.

The gospel—the good news—is that Jesus took our place, accepting the punishment for our sin and making peace between us and God (see 2 Cor. 5:21). But Jesus does more than pay for our sin. He helps us live each day in the freedom and joy of our salvation. No matter what we're going through, Immanuel is with us.

Prayer

Heavenly Father, increase my awareness of the beautiful truth that Jesus Christ is fully God and fully man. Thank You that He's both my perfect substitute and my perfect Savior. Help me acknowledge His lordship through greater obedience to Your commands. In the name of Jesus Christ, my Lord. Amen.

DAY 2

While it's difficult, if not impossible, to fully wrap our finite minds around the reality that Jesus is 100 percent God and 100 percent man, the glorious mystery of God's love for us is revealed in Christ. As the second Person of the Trinity, the Son has made a way for us to become children of God.

READ COLOSSIANS 1:15-20.

List the words and descriptions these verses use to emphasize the unique personhood of Jesus Christ.

READ MATTHEW 16:13-17.

How would you answer if Jesus asked you the same question He asked Peter, "Who do you say that I am?" (v. 15)? Record your response.

Peter recognized that there was more to Jesus than people saw. The word *Christ* means "Anointed One" or "Chosen One." It has the same meaning as the Greek word for *Messiah,* the Savior who was predicted throughout the Old Testament. God opened Peter's eyes to this reality. Peter's affirmation was more than factual. It was personal. It was relational.

Nobody can believe for you. It's not enough to know what other people believe about Jesus. The conversation with Peter points out that a lot of people can believe good things about Jesus but can still be wrong about who He truly is.

Other than the Christ and the Son of God, what opinions, good or bad, have you heard about Jesus?

The Bible includes another conversation between Jesus and His disciples about His identity and a relationship with God. Once again, Jesus used familial language.

READ JOHN 14:1-6.

Notice that Jesus said, "I am *the* way, and *the* truth, and *the* life" and was then unmistakably clear: *"No one* comes to the Father except through me" (v. 6, emphasis added). The Apostles' Creed is also exclusive and definitive in its wording: *His only* Son.

Jesus may be popular and often well respected, but belief in Jesus as the only way to truly know God and to live eternally in heaven is as divisive now as it was when Jesus spoke these words.

If you believe in Jesus as the only Son of God, the only way to know the truth about God, and the only way to eternal life in heaven, then what other religious or philosophical beliefs can't be true?

READ JOHN 14:15.

Faith in Jesus is more than agreeing that He's fully God and fully man. Belief in Jesus is even more than agreeing that He's the only way to know God and to live with Him forever. Saving faith is belief that leads to action.

Think about the different things going on in your life. What do you need to do to obey Jesus in each area of your life?

Prayer

Spend time declaring the truth about Jesus, praising Him for who He is and what He's done for you. Thank God for revealing to you the truth about His only Son.

DAY 3

Christian belief is more than an opinion about Jesus. It's surrender to His lordship as Savior and King. He's the promised Messiah, the only One who can save us. Therefore, He's worthy of our lives.

Early Christians who professed Jesus as Lord were doing more than declaring a religious affiliation; they were declaring allegiance to only Jesus' authority. The Roman law required everyone to acknowledge Caesar as Lord. Christians who proclaimed that Jesus was Lord were singled out as disloyal to Rome and the prevailing culture. Their disobedience brought condemnation and persecution. Furthermore, the Jewish culture rejected belief in Jesus as the Christ and the only Son of God. To believe otherwise was to be rejected by the religious community. Professing the lordship of Christ is central to the gospel in every age because in doing so, Christians declare that Jesus is the true King and Lord of all.

The statement "I believe in ... Jesus Christ, His only Son, our Lord" brings symmetry, clarity, community, and counsel to the Christian life and witness.

1. SYMMETRY

Time for a gut check. Legitimate, life-or-death persecution has been a part of Christianity since Jesus was crucified. Millions of Christians live with the reality of persecution right now. Though it may be easy to say you're committed to your faith in Jesus, consider your life. Are you claiming Jesus as your Savior with no submission to Him as Lord? This is a foreign concept in the Bible. It's a lie of our convenience-based consumer culture to believe we can have the benefits of salvation without paying a cost for following Jesus.

2. CLARITY

If Jesus is who He says He is, you can't be indifferent to that claim. Is He the way, the truth, and the life or not (see John 14:6)? Is He the only Son, fully God and fully man, or not? Is He the Savior and Lord or not? Like the disciples, you must decide what you believe about Jesus. To be clear, deciding what you believe doesn't mean deciding whether it's true. Truth is truth. You're responsible for what you'll do now that you've heard the truth about Jesus.

> **How well do your actions line up with what you say you believe about Jesus? Mark a point on the scale that represents your answer.**
>
> | 1 | 2 | 3 | 4 | 5 | 6 | 7 | 8 | 9 | 10 |
> |---|---|---|---|---|---|---|---|---|---|
> | **Not at all** | | | | | | | | | **Completely** |

READ MATTHEW 7:21-23.

These are some of the most sobering words in Scripture. We can't take faith and obedience lightly. They're inseparable parts of the Christian life. For Christ to be Savior, He must also be Lord. There's no middle ground. Jesus said we're either in or we're out. If we merely pay lip service and don't submit to Him as King, then we're not a part of His kingdom.

3. COMMUNITY

When you declare, "Jesus is Lord," you join the voices of every believer from the past two thousand years and around the world today. You join your brothers and sisters in Christ. The Apostles' Creed is specific when it says Jesus Christ is "our Lord," not just "the Lord." A confession of personal faith is a commitment to the community of faith.

4. COUNSEL

Jesus said to believe in Him and that He will return when our eternal home is ready (see John 14:1-6). He's coming back. When He does, He's coming for those in true relationship with Him. We've been given the truth. We must live each day for the sake of Jesus Christ, the only Son of God, our Lord.

READ 2 CORINTHIANS 5:16-21.

Prayer

Ask God to give you a desperate burden for reconciliation
with Him. In prayer repent of your sin, submitting to Christ as Lord.
Also pray that God will equally burden you with a sense of urgency
for others to be reconciled with Him through saving faith in Jesus.

Week Four

I believe in God the Father Almighty,
    Creator of heaven and earth,
And in Jesus Christ, His only Son, our Lord,
Who was conceived by the Holy Spirit;
    born of the virgin Mary;
Suffered under Pontius Pilate;
    was crucified, dead, and buried.
He descended to hell; the third day
    He rose again from the dead;
He ascended to heaven and sits on the
    right hand of the Father Almighty,
From whence He shall come to judge
    the living and the dead.
I believe in the Holy Spirit,
The holy catholic church,
    the communion of saints,
The forgiveness of sins,
The resurrection of the body,
    and the life everlasting. Amen.

Group Study

START

WHO WAS CONCEIVED BY THE HOLY SPIRIT; BORN OF THE VIRGIN MARY

Welcome everyone to week 4 of The Apostles' Creed.
Use this page to begin the group session.

Let's begin by taking a few minutes to review last week's study.

What was the most meaningful or challenging part of your personal study or family discipleship from "And in Jesus Christ, His only Son, our Lord"? What did you learn or experience in a specific way this week?

Day 3 focused on the grid for understanding and applying each of the core doctrines summarized in the Apostles' Creed. Which of the four areas were most applicable this week and why? (Refer to pp. 44–45 if needed.)

1. Symmetry: a balanced, robust understanding of biblical teaching
2. Clarity: a picture of who God truly is, not who we want Him to be
3. Community: an understanding of how to relate to one another as Christians
4. Counsel: an ability to speak biblical truth to ourselves and to others

The foundation of all our beliefs is a right understanding of God. The Apostles' Creed begins by introducing the triune God of the Bible. The Christian faith is monotheistic, meaning we believe in and worship one true God. We also believe this one true God exists in three distinct but equal Persons: Father, Son, and Holy Spirit. In week 9 we'll focus more on the Person and work of the Holy Spirit, but this week we'll introduce this mysterious and therefore most misunderstood Person of the Trinity by showing how the Holy Spirit was involved in the birth of Christ through the virgin Mary.

Read the Apostles' Creed aloud as a group
before watching video session 4.

WATCH

*Use this viewer guide to follow along and
take notes as you watch video session 4.*

Sin can be an outright rejection of how God designed the universe to work.

Some of us sin by using religion to not need God.

The triune God of the universe—God the Father, God the Son, God the Holy Spirit, three in one—is after the hearts of men.

God is an initiating God.

God pushes out impossibilities.

1. SYMMETRY

The theme of the Bible is not that the world's not messy but that God's at work in the mess.

2. CLARITY

The more you understand that you did not save you but God saved you, the more confident you'll be in God of your salvation.

3. COMMUNITY

We should be a community of optimists, and we should stand in contrast to the pessimism of the world around us.

4. COUNSEL

The confession underneath a lot of other statements is "I don't trust God."

God doesn't despise the confession of "I don't trust You" if it's coming from a broken heart.

DISCUSS

Discuss the video segment, using the following questions.

READ LUKE 1:26-38.

Why is it important, not only in this story but also in our lives, to know that our God initiates a relationship with His people?

How does Mary's response exemplify faith in a God who overcomes impossibilities?

When have you questioned God's work in the midst of a difficult or confusing situation? How has God proved Himself throughout Scripture to work in the midst of a mess rather than simply remove the mess?

Why would Matt say it gives you confidence in your salvation to believe that you didn't save yourself but rather that God saved you?

Have you ever questioned your salvation, or do you currently doubt your salvation? Why do you think you doubt your salvation?

How would you define Christian optimism? How is this idea a testimony and contrast to the world? Why is pessimism easy?

What's a practical example of a sin or a doubt that ultimately boils down to "I don't trust God"?

In what area of your life do you need to confess a lack of trust in God?

What's your primary observation about the teaching on "Who was conceived by the Holy Spirit; born of the virgin Mary"?

What remaining thoughts or questions do you have?

Encourage members to complete the following personal studies before the next group session.

Family Discipleship

ENGAGE

The Apostles' Creed presents a great opportunity for families to consider the truths of the gospel together by utilizing the following framework for family discipleship: time, moments, and milestones.

- ☐ **TIME. Continue memorizing the Apostles' Creed as a family. Look for opportunities for each person to practice what you've learned so far. Say the lines together before you pray for a meal or at bedtime.**

- ☐ **MOMENTS. As your family interacts with or sees babies and young children, use those opportunities to talk about what Jesus was like as a baby, a toddler, and a child. Jesus cried as a baby, started to smile, learned to roll over, took His first step, and said His first word just as we did. Yet Jesus, though fully human, was and is also fully God. Jesus knows what it's like to be human and, at the same time, is worthy of all honor, worship, trust, and obedience.**

- ☐ **MILESTONES. Look ahead to the Christmas holiday. As a family, consider one new tradition you can incorporate into your celebration of the Advent season to help your family remember the significance of Jesus' incarnation. Consider giving your children gifts of spiritual significance that can remind them of the work of Jesus Christ.**

MEMORIZE

*Use this page to practice writing
the Apostles' Creed from memory.*

Personal Study

DAY 1

The presence and activity of God are established in the opening words of Scripture (see Gen. 1:1). Throughout the Bible we read of God's miraculous work as what the creed has summarized as "the Father Almighty." He's infinitely powerful yet intensely personal.

READ EXODUS 40:34-38.

In the Old Testament the glory of the Lord was seen as a cloud that rested on the tabernacle, the portable temple of God's people, the place where they worshiped God. This visible representation of the glory of the Lord was called the *shekinah*. In Ezekiel 10 the prophet Ezekiel saw the glory of the Lord, the shekinah, leave the temple, but Ezekiel also had a vision of God's glory returning to a new temple, recorded in Ezekiel 43:1-5.

READ LUKE 1:35.

The Bible says the Holy Spirit would "overshadow" Mary to enable her to conceive a son. In the Greek translation of the Old Testament, the same word for *overshadow* is used to describe the cloud of God's glory in Exodus 40:35, where the Bible says, "Moses was not able to enter the tent of meeting because the cloud settled on it, and the glory of the LORD [shekinah] filled the tabernacle."

Luke connected the shekinah glory of God to the conception of Jesus. His overwhelmingly glorious presence in the tabernacle and the temple now manifested itself through Mary as she conceived, carried, and gave birth to her firstborn child, the only Son of God.

What do you think would be lost if the creed said "born of the virgin Mary?" without saying "conceived by the Holy Spirit"?

The Scriptures are full of miraculous births of people meant for specific purposes: Sarah and Abraham had Isaac, the promised child and head of God's covenant people (see Gen. 18:9-14); Jacob and Rachel had Joseph, the royal savior (see Gen. 30:22-24); Manoah and his wife had Samson, the judge (see Judg. 13); Elkanah and Hannah had Samuel, the prophet (see 1 Sam. 1); and Zechariah and Elizabeth had John the Baptist, the preacher of repentance and the kingdom of God (see

Luke 1:5-25,57-63). In each of these cases, the Lord opened barren wombs and provided a child when none seemed possible—although the woman conceived with her husband. In each case the unexpected birth was foretold. In the Book of Isaiah, the prophet Isaiah characterized Israel as a barren woman longing for children and prophesied that she would one day be a mother (see Isa. 66:7-14).

How did each of the miraculous births in Scripture point to Jesus?

All of history had been leading up to Jesus. The opening chapter of John's Gospel uses the same language as the creation account in Genesis, words like *in the beginning, light, darkness,* and *world.* John was clearly pointing to Jesus as the Almighty, the Creator, Christ, and Lord as the only Son of God. Then John gave a beautiful picture of the supernatural birth.

READ JOHN 1:14.

The Greek word John used for *dwelt* means "to tabernacle." God has tabernacled with us through the birth of Jesus, making His glory known to the world.

In what ways has God made Himself known to you?

How does it change your life to know that God wants to be with you?

Prayer

Father, You're truly the God of the universe. You're so much bigger, so much more glorious than I can understand. Thank You for caring so intimately for me, even in all Your majesty, that You sent Your Son to become flesh and blood for my sake. Holy Spirit, help my heart remember and be comforted in knowing that I have a God who truly empathizes with me in every way and loves me enough to dwell among people. Amen.

DAY 2

In the birth of Jesus, we see God entering our world in a beautiful and unexpected way. An early church theologian named Athanasius described God's incarnation this way: "He entered the world in a new way, stooping to our level in His love and Self-revealing to us."[1]

When Athanasius said Christ stooped to our level in the incarnation, he reminded us that God condescended, voluntarily put aside His superiority, and made Himself equal with us, as inferior as we are to the Almighty, in order to have communion with us. The very God of the universe humbled Himself by taking on Himself total humanity in its weakest form, a baby.

READ PHILIPPIANS 2:3-8.

Identify and list the words used to describe Christ's humility.

Like faith, humility is ultimately demonstrated in obedience to God. Jesus humbled Himself in obedience to God. Verse 6 says He "did not count equality with God a thing to be grasped." This means Jesus didn't cling to His position of honor, holding Himself above the will of God. It wasn't beneath Him to live and die as a man even though He was and is part of the triune God.

Look at the story of Mary to see Christlike humility. To be clear, the Bible doesn't give any explanation for why God chose Mary. Like us all, she was a sinner in need of a Savior (see Luke 1:47). Scripture doesn't say she was rewarded for her godliness, but we see her humble obedience demonstrated in her response to God's grace.

READ LUKE 1:26-38.

Put yourself in Mary's place. She was a young girl, most likely barely in her teens, engaged to be married, and an angel appeared to tell her that she was going to be pregnant. If that wasn't shocking enough, Mary would become pregnant while remaining a virgin, and the baby would be the Son of God. Surely no one in history had ever been more surprised.

Notice in Mary's response to the angel that she was afraid (see v. 29), she had questions (see v. 34), yet she submitted herself to God's will in humble obedience (see v. 38).

What about complete obedience to God frightens you?

What questions do you have about living by faith?

In what areas of your life are you most prone to pride?

What will you do so that Mary's words become the posture of your heart?

I am the servant of the Lord; let it be to me according to your word.
LUKE 1:38

Prayer

Holy Spirit of God, thank You for making my heart new and united with Christ. Thank You that my union with Him reminds me that You've chosen the weak things of the world, including the Messiah born of a virgin, to shame the wisdom of the wise. In the incarnation, Christ, You stooped to my level in order to reveal Yourself to me. Make me Your ambassador and proclaimer of this beautiful gospel message. Amen.

1. Saint Athanasius of Alexandria, as quoted in *Christian Doctrine,* ed. Lindsey Hall, Murray Rae, and Steven Holmes (London: SCM, 2010), 176.

DAY 3

Popular culture often looks down on ideas and events that seem as irrational and unbelievable as the virgin birth. Some say science and culture have progressed to a point that we can leave supernatural beliefs behind in favor of what can be proved, observed, and repeated. However, the Bible is full of miraculous accounts.

Ultimately, as a Christian, you must decide whether you believe in an almighty God who has authority and power over all creation. If the God of the Bible exists, miracles are simply part of the deal; that's just part of how an almighty Creator works. It's quite logical to conclude that a supernatural God works in supernatural ways. It's His nature.

Nothing will be impossible with God.
LUKE 1:37

Do you believe these words of the angel who spoke to Mary?

YES   NO   NOT SURE

Belief in the virgin birth is essential in shaping the Christian life. It testifies to the nature of Jesus as both God and man, as well as to the fact that we have an all-powerful Father who interacts with His creation to make Himself known. Many, if not most, difficulties with or objections to believing in God are more about ourselves and our circumstances than they are about God. Take a look at the story of a father who was in a difficult situation but was learning how to believe. Then answer the following questions about the four areas addressed in the group session.

READ MARK 9:14-29.

1. SYMMETRY

What difficult, painful, or hopeless situation are you facing that seems as if it would take a miracle to change for the better?

2. CLARITY

Just as the disciples were unable to save the boy, we're completely dependent on Jesus' miraculous work in our lives. We've already seen that Christ is the only way to experience true and eternal life. We can't be good enough, try hard enough, have good enough intentions, or know the right things to say or do to attain eternal life on our own. Salvation is the greatest miracle of all, transforming sinful people into the righteousness of Christ (see 2 Cor. 5:21). All other miracles point to the person and work of Jesus Christ.

How have you experienced God's work in your life to accomplish things you could never do for yourself?

3. COMMUNITY

In what ways do you struggle with pessimism? How can you set an example for the people around you by believing that anything is possible with God and that no situation is hopeless?

4. COUNSEL

Consider the areas of pessimism and bad attitudes in your life. In what specific ways do those attitudes reveal a lack of faith in God's ability to work in those circumstances?

Prayer

Reflect on the confession and plea of the father
in Mark 9:24. Cry out to God, making this your prayer.
Be specific about the areas in which you need to trust Him.
I believe; help my unbelief!
MARK 9:24

Week Five

I believe in God the Father Almighty,
    Creator of heaven and earth,
And in Jesus Christ, His only Son, our Lord,
Who was conceived by the Holy Spirit;
    born of the virgin Mary;
Suffered under Pontius Pilate;
    was crucified, dead, and buried.
He descended to hell; the third day
    He rose again from the dead;
He ascended to heaven and sits on the
    right hand of the Father Almighty,
From whence He shall come to judge
    the living and the dead.
I believe in the Holy Spirit,
The holy catholic church,
    the communion of saints,
The forgiveness of sins,
The resurrection of the body,
    and the life everlasting. Amen.

Group Study

START

SUFFERED UNDER PONTIUS PILATE; WAS CRUCIFIED, DEAD, AND BURIED

Welcome everyone to week 5 of The Apostles' Creed. *Use this page to begin the group session.*

Let's begin by taking a few minutes to review last week's study.

What was the most meaningful or challenging part of your personal study or family discipleship from "Who was conceived by the Holy Spirit; born of the virgin Mary"? What did you learn or experience in a specific way this week?

Day 3 focused on the grid for understanding and applying each of the core doctrines summarized in the Apostles' Creed. Which of the four areas were most applicable this week and why? (Refer to pp. 56–57 if needed.)

1. Symmetry: a balanced, robust understanding of biblical teaching
2. Clarity: a picture of who God truly is, not who we want Him to be
3. Community: an understanding of how to relate to one another as Christians
4. Counsel: an ability to speak biblical truth to ourselves and to others

Last week we studied the birth of Jesus. This week we'll see why He was born: Jesus' incarnation was necessary for His crucifixion. He was born to die, but He died so that we could truly live.

Read the Apostles' Creed aloud as a group before watching video session 5.

WATCH

*Use this viewer guide to follow along and
take notes as you watch video session 5.*

The death of Christ reconciles us to God.

The death of Jesus purchases a people, creates the church.

1. SYMMETRY
The death of Jesus helps you understand how much God hates sin—all sin.

2. CLARITY
If you are in Christ, you are fully and completely forgiven.

There is no sin imaginable with more power than the cross of Jesus Christ.

3. COMMUNITY
The death of Jesus Christ is the bedrock upon which our community is built.

4. COUNSEL
The love of Christ is free.

The cross is a visceral, visible picture of the love of God for you in Christ.

The joy set before Christ in the cross was in glorifying God.

You and I are the joy set before Christ on that day.

You get to stop striving and rest in the accomplished work of Jesus Christ.

Video sessions available at lifeway.com/apostlescreed

DISCUSS

Discuss the video segment, using the following questions.

How did it make you feel when Matt said despite what we may feel, the truth is that in Christ, God is pleased when He looks at us?

READ JOHN 18:36-38.

What did Jesus say He had come into the world to do?

Why is it important to believe in Jesus as more than an abstract, philosophical idea but rather as the Truth of God incarnate?

Why is it significant for the creed to emphasize the biblical accounts of Jesus' suffering, crucifixion, death, and burial as historical facts?

How is the cross a picture of God's love for us? How is it a picture of God's hatred of all sin? What sins do we treat as more or less hated by God?

What did Matt mean when he said, "There is no sin imaginable with more power than the cross of Jesus Christ"? If we believe no sin has more power than the cross, why do we struggle with feeling forgiven? With giving forgiveness?

Why is the death of Jesus foundational for Christian community?

In what ways are you striving to feel lovable and worthy rather than accepting the free gift of grace through faith in Jesus?

What does it look like for you to rest in the accomplished work of Christ?

What's your primary observation about the teaching on "Suffered under Pontius Pilate; was crucified, dead, and buried"?

What remaining thoughts or questions do you have?

Encourage members to complete the following personal studies before the next group session.

Family Discipleship

ENGAGE

The Apostles' Creed presents a great opportunity for families to consider the truths of the gospel together by utilizing the following framework for family discipleship: time, moments, and milestones.

☐ **TIME. Continue memorizing the Apostles' Creed as a family. Look for opportunities for each person in your household to practice what you've learned so far. Say this week's statement together before you pray at a meal or at bedtime.**

☐ **MOMENTS. Capitalize on moments of suffering, discouragement, or tough discipline to point out God's good work, even in times of suffering. Read and connect Romans 8:28 to family members' hurt, emphasizing that God took on our suffering through Christ's obedient, victorious death.**

☐ **MILESTONES. The death of a friend or a loved one is an important, though difficult, milestone to mark for a family. If your family has suffered loss, consider ways to remember the people you've lost on special days throughout the year, such as birthdays, major holidays, or the anniversaries of their passing. Believers know death doesn't have the final say. Point to the hope of Christ and the promise of eternal life as you remember your loved ones.**

MEMORIZE

*Use this page to practice writing
the Apostles' Creed from memory.*

Personal Study

DAY 1

Suffering is an inevitable part of the human experience. The degrees of suffering might differ from person to person, but everyone experiences periods of suffering. Physical ailments, emotional calamity, and spiritual crises can all cause suffering.

Reflect on times in your life when you suffered. What specific experiences come to mind when you think about suffering?

Consider the intensity, duration, or type of suffering you've experienced. What emotions, thoughts, or questions have you had when suffering?

READ ISAIAH 52:14; 53:4-5.

These verses prophesy the suffering Jesus would endure in His crucifixion. List the words used in these verses to describe Jesus' suffering.

READ MATTHEW 27:24-26.

Pontius Pilate was the governor of Judea from A.D. 26 to 36. This mention of Pilate in the Apostles' Creed may seem odd, but it highlights Christ's suffering as a historical event. The eternal Son entered our world, and a human court convicted Him of crimes He didn't commit. This event really happened. Jesus, fully human, experienced real suffering at a specific point in history.

How are you comforted in your suffering by the fact that Christ experienced true, intense suffering?

Why is it important for faith to be rooted in historical facts? How does it change your perspective in day-to-day events—especially in suffering—not only to look to the future in faith but also to remember what Christ has already done for you?

READ ROMANS 5:1-11.

List the words used to describe in past tense what Christ has done for you.

Believing in Christ doesn't exempt you from suffering. In fact, some suffering may result because of your faith (see John 15:18-21).

What hope do you have as a Christian in the midst of suffering?

Prayer

Jesus, thank You for paying the price for my sins and for dying the death I deserve. The cross is a reminder of Your love for me. Continue to transform my life and make me more like You. I love You because You first loved me. Amen.

DAY 2

The crucifixion was the ultimate display of human animosity toward God's authority in our lives. Our sinful hearts rejected Christ, in spite of all His displays of love, because we hated His claim of lordship. If He's the rightful King over our lives, we must confess and repent of our rebellion, surrendering our lives in submission to His rule. But instead, we demanded that Jesus be executed.

READ MATTHEW 27.

How does the crucifixion highlight the ugliness of sin in your heart? What thoughts or feelings did you experience as you read this chapter?

In what ways are you prone to demand what you want, resisting the idea that Jesus is the Lord of everything?

God wasn't surprised by the world's hatred and rejection of Jesus. And Jesus didn't suffer and die in a way that was out of His control. Before the crucifixion He told His disciples:

> *No one takes [my life] from me, but I lay it down of my own accord.*
> *I have authority to lay it down, and I have authority to take it up again.*
> **JOHN 10:18**

The Roman Empire asserted control through brutal practices like crucifixion, a form of execution reserved for people who posed a threat to Rome. Often the condemned were crucified along busy roads as reminders that Rome had power over life and death. But the apostle Paul said the rulers and authorities who crucified Him were ultimately put to shame (see Col. 2:13-15). Jesus' apparent defeat was a victory, and He triumphed over those who were trying to conquer Him. His willingness to suffer and die was the ultimate act of love for all people who put their faith in Him.

The Father gave His Son to suffer our punishment for our sins. From His love for all humanity, Jesus, who never committed sin, became sin for us (see 2 Cor. 5:21).

The resurrection demonstrated that the Father accepted Jesus' payment for our sin, and it also demonstrated Jesus' authority over life and death. Therefore, God accepts us as forgiven and justified in His sight.

READ ROMANS 3:10-26.

Why did we need a sacrificial substitute to take our place on the cross?

How do these verses address both judgment and grace?

READ ROMANS 5:6-11.

List all the descriptions used for people apart from the work of Jesus.

In light of the Scriptures you've read today that emphasize the sin and hopelessness of life apart from Christ, how can you rejoice? What does the death of Jesus make possible?

Prayer

Jesus, thank You for dying for my sins. In Your death You've reconciled me to the Father. My life is changed forever because of Your love for me. I want to be like You and live in this world in such a way that my allegiance to You is evident in the way I love You and others. Please be gracious to me as You enable me to live to that end. Amen.

DAY 3

From the beginning of history, sin has required death as its penalty. God warned Adam that disobedience—eating the fruit—would result in inevitable death (see Gen. 2:17). In the garden God's judgment and grace were seen in the literal covering of Adam's shame by the skin of an animal, a sacrificial death (see 3:21). Immediately following the fall of humanity, the sons of Adam offered sacrifices to God, and He warned about the deadly effects of sin (see 4:3-7). From the time of Adam until the time of Jesus, sacrifice was a part of the relationship between God and His people.

READ ROMANS 5:12-21.

Jesus' death and resurrection changed everything. We can now have a right relationship with God again. Our disobedience, our sin, and our rebellion as His enemies are all forgiven. No amount of right or wrong morality, good or bad religious behavior could ever make us right before God. So as He did in the garden after that first sin, God stepped in, sought us, and called us to receive the sacrifice He provided. But the sacrifice of Jesus is infinitely greater than any other offering.

READ HEBREWS 10:1-10.

Based on what you've studied, including the verses from Romans 5 and Hebrews 10, how would you describe the necessity of the cross?

Now let's look at some ways this profound reality changes our lives. Imagine you're having a conversation with a friend. Use the following questions to help you put into your own words a gospel explanation of Jesus' crucifixion.

1. SYMMETRY
If God is a good and loving God, is sin really a serious problem?

2. CLARITY

Are some sins too serious for God to forgive?

3. COMMUNITY

I keep messing up no matter how hard I try to be a good person. If God takes sin so seriously, how could He ever love me?

4. COUNSEL

What do I have to do as a Christian to be forgiven of all my sins? How can I be good enough to repay God for what I've done?

Record a prayer confessing the seriousness of your sin and acknowledging your personal responsibility and your need for Jesus' death. Praise Him for willingly sacrificing His life in your place, setting you free from death and hopelessness.

Week Six

I believe in God the Father Almighty,
    Creator of heaven and earth,
And in Jesus Christ, His only Son, our Lord,
Who was conceived by the Holy Spirit;
    born of the virgin Mary;
Suffered under Pontius Pilate;
    was crucified, dead, and buried.
He descended to hell; the third day
    He rose again from the dead;
He ascended to heaven and sits on the
    right hand of the Father Almighty,
From whence He shall come to judge
    the living and the dead.
I believe in the Holy Spirit,
The holy catholic church,
    the communion of saints,
The forgiveness of sins,
The resurrection of the body,
    and the life everlasting. Amen.

Group Study

START

HE DESCENDED TO HELL; THE THIRD DAY
HE ROSE AGAIN FROM THE DEAD

Welcome everyone to week 6 of The Apostles' Creed.
Use this page to begin the group session.

Let's begin by taking a few minutes to review last week's study.

What was the most meaningful or challenging part of your personal study or family discipleship from "Suffered under Pontius Pilate; was crucified, dead, and buried"? What did you learn or experience in a specific way this week?

Day 3 focused on the grid for understanding and applying each of the core doctrines summarized in the Apostles' Creed. Which of the four areas were most applicable this week and why? (Refer to pp. 68–69 if needed.)

1. Symmetry: a balanced, robust understanding of biblical teaching
2. Clarity: a picture of who God truly is, not who we want Him to be
3. Community: an understanding of how to relate to one another
  as Christians
4. Counsel: an ability to speak biblical truth to ourselves and to others

The death, burial, and resurrection of Jesus are essential beliefs of the Christian faith as well as historical events. This week's phrases in the Apostles' Creed emphasize the fact that Jesus fully experienced death on our behalf before being raised from the dead. The inclusion of hell in the creed is controversial and debated among Christians, but we'll see why it's an important part of what we believe to be true about the gospel of Jesus Christ.

Read the Apostles' Creed aloud as a group
before watching video session 6.

WATCH

Use this viewer guide to follow along and take notes as you watch video session 6.

Separation from God—that's the hell that Christ experiences.

Hell is the absence of the presence of God to bless and is simply the presence of God to judge.

The resurrection of Jesus Christ was a bodily, physical resurrection.

Because Christ is not dead, our confidence is that all of our sins have been forgiven.

We experience a spiritual resurrection. We are dead in our sins, and we are made alive in the resurrection of Christ.

There will be a physical resurrection from the dead.

1. SYMMETRY

Being sealed by the Holy Spirit of God invites you into the freedom that's reserved for the children of God.

2. CLARITY

Christ freely went to the cross; Christ knew what He was buying.

3. COMMUNITY

The resurrected, bodily Jesus continues to extend the invitation.

We live powerfully in the present with our hope on the glory of the future.

4. COUNSEL

Don't fear the ongoing ethics of the Christian walk: confession, repentance, and honesty.

DISCUSS

Discuss the video segment, using the following questions.

What's your reaction to Matt's description of the phrase "He descended to hell"?

How does this phrase give weight to our own sinfulness?

Why is it vital to the gospel that Jesus fully experienced death?

Why is it vital to the gospel that Jesus was physically resurrected?

READ EPHESIANS 2:1-5.

What false sense of freedom does the world pursue apart from Jesus?

How does this Scripture passage describe the human condition before Christ? What power brings destruction in our broken world and human hearts?

How would you describe the freedom of being a child of God? How can conversion be summed up in the hellish reality of death, followed by the miraculous triumph of resurrection?

Why are God's sovereignty and omniscience essential to understanding Jesus' atoning work on the cross?

Why do we fear confession, repentance, and honesty?

Why must these realities be part of our ongoing Christian walk, not just part of our initial conversion?

What's your primary observation about the teaching on "He descended to hell; the third day He rose again from the dead"?

What remaining thoughts or questions do you have?

Encourage members to complete the following personal studies before the next group session.

Family Discipleship

ENGAGE

The Apostles' Creed presents a great opportunity for families to consider the truths of the gospel together by utilizing the following framework for family discipleship: time, moments, and milestones.

- ☐ **TIME. Continue memorizing the Apostles' Creed as a family. Practice it together before you pray at a meal or before bed. Consider talking about what you've learned in the creed so far.**

- ☐ **MOMENTS. Many children are naturally curious about death and are often very afraid of it. Look for opportunities to point out that Jesus' resurrection showed that He's stronger than both sin and death. That means people who love and trust Him don't need to fear death, because Jesus is always with us.**

- ☐ **MILESTONES. Look ahead to ways you'll celebrate Easter in the coming year. Think of one new tradition your family can incorporate into your celebration of Jesus' resurrection.**

MEMORIZE

*Use this page to practice writing
the Apostles' Creed from memory.*

Personal Study

DAY 1

Let's go ahead and address the elephant in the room. For some people, the phrase "He descended to hell" is controversial. This phrase wasn't included in the earliest forms of the Apostles' Creed but was added by a Roman theologian named Rufinus in A.D. 390.

Rufinus didn't interpret the phrase to mean that Jesus went to a place of eternal judgment but rather that Jesus went down into the earth and was buried. Christ, in His humanity, fully experienced death and judgment for sin on our behalf. His burial was a vicarious, victorious one because He descended into the grave, into the earth He created. By doing so, Jesus experienced death with us and for us. He also defeated death for us and was resurrected, as we shall be someday.

READ MATTHEW 12:38-40.

What did Jesus say would be the great sign or miracle proving that He was the only Son of God?

Why does it matter that Jesus fully experienced death and the grave for us and because of us?

How would your understanding of the gospel change if Jesus hadn't personally taken on our punishment by going to the place of death for us?

READ 1 CORINTHIANS 15:12-19.

What did Paul say about the relationship between the resurrection of Jesus and the resurrection of all people? Can you believe in one but not the other? Why or why not?

If there were no forgiveness of sin and eternal life, but believing in Jesus still made us better moral people, what did Paul conclude about such a faith (see v. 19)? What did he mean?

READ 1 CORINTHIANS 15:20-23.

The Bible often uses agricultural terms such as *firstfruits,* a word that describes the part of the harvest that's offered in thanks to God for His provision. When wheat begins to ripen in a field, it signals that soon the whole harvest will be ready.

What did Paul mean when He said Jesus is the firstfruits of the resurrection (see v. 20)?

What's Paul's conclusion, based on the fact that Jesus was resurrected?

Prayer

Father, thank You for sending Jesus to die on my behalf, to descend into the grave where I deserve to be because of my sin. Thank You for raising Him from the dead, thereby demonstrating that He's Your eternal Son; that my sins have been paid for; and that He's the righteous Messiah, sent to show me the way to eternal life. Holy Spirit, remind my heart of these truths and remind me that one day, like my Savior, Jesus Christ, I'll be bodily raised as well. I ask this in Jesus' name. Amen.

DAY 2

Socrates once said, "Death may be the greatest of all human blessings."[1] He meant death brings peace from the ailments of human life. But is this true? Death is normal, but is it good or even natural?

Death isn't part of the purpose we were created for. The benefit of death, such as getting to be with Jesus, is good but not death itself. Humans were made to live with God forever and not to die. Death is a curse. All of us, as descendants of Adam and Eve, have been affected by the curse of death.

Think about ways death has affected your life. Whom have you lost? Do you have hope that they'll be raised with Christ to eternal life?

How does the reality of heaven, hell, and resurrection affect your thoughts and feelings about death? How does it affect your sense of urgency in sharing the gospel?

Identify people you know who need to respond in faith to the life, death, and resurrection of Jesus Christ.

READ 2 CORINTHIANS 5.

What perspective did Paul have on our purpose in life?

Biblically, the first step of faith and obedience in the Christian life is one marked by death. We join every believer since Pentecost by identifying with Christ and one another through baptism (see Acts 2:41). As Paul wrote, "The old has passed away; behold, the new has come" (2 Cor. 5:17). Our public identification with Jesus in baptism is a picture of being fully united with Christ in His death and descent into the grave and His subsequent resurrection with a new body.

READ ROMANS 6:1-11.

What's the significance of Paul's words "We were buried therefore with him" and "We too might walk in newness of life" (v. 4)? How does the resurrection change the way you live day to day?

When were you baptized? Describe the experience and the significance. Talk to someone this week about the significance of your baptism.

If your baptism was an identification with Christ, dying to your sin and receiving new life in Him, share that good news with someone. If you haven't been baptized, if you've been baptized but weren't sure what it meant, or if you have any other questions, be sure to speak to your leader or someone in your group.

Prayer

Father, I hate death. I love Your original creation that had no stain, no blemish, no sickness, and no death. I praise You because in Christ death has been defeated, and life is now victorious. I adore You, Son of God, who in Your death and resurrection defeated the last enemy—death. Death has literally been left in the grave. I adore You because in Your resurrection You teach me that one day my body that currently suffers will be perfect again. Give me faith and perseverance to long for Your return. I'm waiting for You, Jesus. Come make all things right again by the power of the Spirit. I ask these things in the name of Jesus. Amen.

1. Socrates, as quoted on Thinkexist.com [online, cited 5 December 2016]. Available from the Internet: thinkexist.com.

DAY 3

The resurrection truly makes the Christian faith unique. Throughout history many people have died for their beliefs. Countless martyrs have willingly and even eagerly given their lives for their faith, refusing to compromise their convictions because they were certain the reward for faithfulness was greater than any suffering they endured. The difference between Jesus and any guru, prophet, teacher, leader, or hero is that He was the only Son of God and didn't stay dead. Jesus not only suffered and died but also rose from His burial place, left the tomb empty, and appeared before hundreds of eyewitnesses.

The resurrection of Jesus is not only miraculous but also evidence that only He has authority over life and death and the ability to forgive sin. Because Christ isn't dead, we can be confident that all our sins have been forgiven.

How do these truths strengthen your faith and make Christianity unique?

READ 1 CORINTHIANS 15:3-11.

Why did Paul record different witnesses to the resurrection at different times? Why is it significant that over five hundred people saw Jesus at the same time?

Paul said some of the witnesses had fallen asleep. Sleep is a common euphemism for death, but it has theological significance.

READ ISAIAH 26:19 AND DANIEL 12:2.

What do these verses say about physical death? About eternity?

One of the great but overlooked promises of the Christian faith is the fact that eternal life isn't just a spiritual reality; it's a physical reality. Believers in Christ can look forward to their resurrections and renewed bodies.

With this promise in mind, what's currently broken in you that will be restored (physical, emotional, psychological, or spiritual ailments)?

When we affirm the words of the Apostles' Creed, we embrace the difficult reality of death and the promise of resurrection. In the words "He descended to hell; the third day He rose again from the dead" we gain an eternal perspective. Let's reflect on our four points of perspective as we pray.

Prayer

1. SYMMETRY

Pray that God will help you live in the freedom of knowing that your eternal salvation has been secured through the death and resurrection of Jesus Christ.

2. CLARITY

Thank God that Jesus laid down His life for you, fully experiencing life and death and becoming your sin so that you could be made new in His righteousness.

3. COMMUNITY

Ask God for opportunities to encourage others in their faith and to invite people to join the family of God through faith in His only Son—our Savior and Lord.

4. COUNSEL

Continually remind yourself of the gospel. Confess any and all sin and repent, putting off the old self and putting on the new self by the grace of Jesus Christ.

Week Seven

I believe in God the Father Almighty,
  Creator of heaven and earth,
And in Jesus Christ, His only Son, our Lord,
Who was conceived by the Holy Spirit;
  born of the virgin Mary;
Suffered under Pontius Pilate;
  was crucified, dead, and buried.
He descended to hell; the third day
  He rose again from the dead;
He ascended to heaven and sits on the
  right hand of the Father Almighty,
From whence He shall come to judge
  the living and the dead.
I believe in the Holy Spirit,
The holy catholic church,
  the communion of saints,
The forgiveness of sins,
The resurrection of the body,
  and the life everlasting. Amen.

Group Study

START

HE ASCENDED TO HEAVEN AND SITS ON THE RIGHT HAND OF THE FATHER ALMIGHTY

Welcome everyone to week 7 of The Apostles' Creed.
Use this page to begin the group session.

Let's begin by taking a few minutes to review last week's study.

What was the most meaningful or challenging part of your personal study or family discipleship from "He descended to hell; the third day He rose again from the dead"? What did you learn or experience in a specific way this week?

Day 3 used our grid for understanding and applying each of the core doctrines summarized in the Apostles' Creed as a guide for prayer. Which of the four areas were most applicable this week and why? (Refer to p. 81 if needed.)

1. Symmetry: a balanced, robust understanding of biblical teaching
2. Clarity: a picture of who God truly is, not who we want Him to be
3. Community: an understanding of how to relate to one another as Christians
4. Counsel: an ability to speak biblical truth to ourselves and to others

Jesus not only rose from the grave, conquering sin and the power of hell, but also ascended to heaven. As we saw last week, He fully experienced death and now lives to exercise full authority over life as our sovereign King.

*Read the Apostles' Creed aloud as a group
before watching video session 7.*

WATCH

*Use this viewer guide to follow along and
take notes as you watch video session 7.*

The Holy Spirit is now the presence of Christ everywhere, available to all at any given moment.

Now that the Holy Spirit has come in full, humans are turned into proper vessels for cosmic renewal.

It is in your internal and external difficulties that darkness is pushed back, that fruit is fully formed, and that our lives are transformed and changed.

It's not that we don't enter difficulty but that in difficulty Christ is there, that His presence and power are there to transform and turn us and change us from one degree of glory to the next.

I am not yet where I will be. I am not yet what I will be.

Holy discontentment is "If Christ is an inexhaustible well, then I want more."

1. SYMMETRY
Some of us need the type of holy discontentment that would make us more serious about sin and more hungry for righteousness.

2. CLARITY
The reason the ascension is so beautiful is with clarity now, you can rest in this: He knows. You have not been abandoned.

3. COMMUNITY
We are not yet what we will be.

4. COUNSEL
I will not give in to the paralysis of guilt and shame when I fall short of what I know God has called me to.

In group life and in community life, you'll be surprised at how often it is your weaknesses that encourage and stir up faith in your brothers and sisters.

DISCUSS

Discuss the video segment, using the following questions.

READ ACTS 1:1-11.

What did the ascension, another historical fact, reveal to Jesus' disciples?

What specific instructions did Jesus give to the disciples?

How do the ascension, commission, and gift of the Spirit apply to us today?

What did Matt mean when he used the term *holy discontentment?*

On a scale of 1 to 10 (1 being not at all and 10 being wholeheartedly), how seriously do you regard sin in your life? How hungry are you for righteousness? Explain your answers. What would it take for you to increase your desire for righteousness instead of for sin?

Have you ever thought everything would be easier if you could see, talk to, and literally follow Jesus in person? In what situations do you most wish that Jesus were physically present?

Jesus promised that He hasn't abandoned us. In what way is the ascension a turning point in the life of the church? Why did Jesus say His ascension benefits His followers?

When have you been encouraged by knowing you weren't the only person who has had certain thoughts or experiences? Who could be encouraged by knowing your past or present weaknesses?

What's your primary observation about the teaching on "He ascended to heaven and sits on the right hand of the Father Almighty"?

What remaining thoughts or questions do you have?

*Encourage members to complete the following
personal studies before the next group session.*

Family Discipleship

ENGAGE

The Apostles' Creed presents a great opportunity for families to consider the truths of the gospel together by utilizing the following framework for family discipleship: time, moments, and milestones.

- ☐ **TIME. Continue memorizing the Apostles' Creed as a family. Practice it together in the car, before you pray at a meal, or at bedtime.**

- ☐ **MOMENTS. When your family sees people from other cultures this week, use the opportunity to point to Jesus' call for us to make disciples of all nations (see Matt. 28:18-20). What do you see Jesus doing around the world? What's your family doing to minister to other nations?**

- ☐ **MILESTONES. Consider ways your family is participating in the Great Commission. Think about planning a cross-cultural experience together. It may be taking a trip to another country or going to a part of your community where you'll be the minority. Research ways you can love and serve the people there, partnering with other churches or organizations. Ministering together as a family is powerful and can become an incredible family-discipleship milestone.**

MEMORIZE

*Use this page to practice writing
the Apostles' Creed from memory.*

Personal Study

DAY 1

This portion of the creed invites us to consider the identity of Jesus as our ascended Lord who, from His exalted position at the Father's right hand, is ruling all things.

READ ACTS 1:1-11.

How did Jesus and the two angels in white robes direct the disciples' attention to their present responsibilities?

Why would Jesus present Himself alive before promising the Holy Spirit and commissioning the disciples to be witnesses of the gospel?

As gloriously expressed by this Scripture passage and this section of the creed, the ascension confirms that Jesus is no longer among the dead and never will be again. His power has proved to be greater than anything in this world—even death. The gospel of Jesus and salvation from sin are certain for people who believe in Him.

READ ACTS 2:32-38.

As Peter preached the first Christian sermon, he concluded with the fact that Jesus rose from the dead, ascended to heaven, and sent His Holy Spirit. God had made it known through Scripture, through His Son, and now through His Spirit that Jesus is the Messiah promised by the Old Testament prophets and the reigning Lord of all creation. This passage teaches us that as Jesus sits at the right hand of the Father, He sends or pours out the Holy Spirit. The biblical account of Jesus' ascension to heaven is meant to give us certainty that He's reigning over all creation.

What phrases in this passage emphasize Jesus' authority? Identify each phrase and briefly explain what it communicates.

How do these prophecies and testimonies give you confidence?

Although Jesus ascended to heaven, it's wrong to say that He's not active in the world. Throughout the Book of Acts, Jesus was still working in the world through the Holy Spirit. The same is true today. Through the Holy Spirit, Jesus is at work to empower Christians to be His witnesses. We've received the Spirit in order to know God and to make Him known with boldness.

Like the disciples who were looking to heaven after Jesus' ascension, what do you need to do right now to obey Jesus and to be His witness?

Prayer

Father, I pray to You in the powerful name of the Lord Jesus Christ, who's at Your right hand at this very moment. I praise Your Son because You've exalted Him above all things and because He rules and reigns over all things. I worship and exalt Your Son because He's worthy. I look forward to the day when You'll send Him to us again and everyone in heaven and on earth will confess that He's Lord. Amen.

DAY 2

We often hear about what Jesus has done and what He's going to do; however, it's easy to forget about Jesus' current role in heaven.

It's vital to keep in our hearts and minds what Jesus has done. That's the cornerstone of the gospel, as we've studied in previous weeks. But we also have a future hope that's certain. We'll look more at the future judgment and the reign of Christ in coming weeks. But don't rush past who Christ is right now and what that means for our lives today.

READ HEBREWS 7:23-28.

Verse 25 says Jesus makes intercession for us. Because Jesus ascended to the Father, He speaks to the Father on our behalf as our High Priest. This is why Christians pray in the name of Jesus. We approach God the Father with confidence through Jesus, our intercessor.

Write a definition of *intercession,* either in your own words or from a dictionary.

Describe how Jesus' intercession applies to your relationship with God.

Robert Murray McCheyne, a 19th-century minister in the Church of Scotland, once said:

If I could hear Christ praying for me in the next room,
I would not fear a million enemies. Yet distance
makes no difference; he is praying for me.[1]

How does the knowledge that Christ is praying for you personally give you hope and confidence?

READ ROMANS 8:26-28.

When have you felt at a total loss to express your thoughts, feelings, or needs?

In what specific areas of your life are you glad to know Christ and His Spirit are interceding on your behalf?

An implication of being at the Father's right hand is that Jesus has unique authority and a unique relationship with the Father, one that belongs only to the Son. He shares in all His Father's power and authority. His presence with the Father doesn't make Him absent from the world but uniquely powerful and present by His Spirit.

READ ROMANS 8:9-17.

The Holy Spirit is present and active not only in the world around you but also in you. God the Father, Son, and Holy Spirit is not only sovereign and in control of all things, but He's also making Himself and His will known to you—His child. You've been created and redeemed for greater purposes than the temporary things of the flesh. God knows your deepest desires and needs, and He perfectly satisfies every one. He's good, and He's with you all the time.

Father, I come to You in the name of Your Son, who's exalted with You in glory and majesty. Thank You for making a way for me to approach Your holy presence. There's no other way into Your presence than through Your Son. I love Him because You've given all things over to His sovereign reign and dominion, for all things were created through Him and for Him. Thank You for giving me such a great High Priest who can sympathize with me and intercede for me. I ask that You won't delay in sending Him back to His people, for the sake of our joy and Your glory. I ask all these things in His beautiful name and by the Spirit whom He has generously and abundantly poured out on me. Amen.

1. Robert Murray McCheyne, *The Works of Robert Murray McCheyne* (New York: Robert Carter & Brothers, 1874), 138.

DAY 3

One way you can know Jesus is alive and well is that you can meet and know Him. Or course, if you're in Christ, you already know this.

Athanasius, a fourth-century Christian theologian, wrote:

> *We are agreed that a dead person can do nothing:*
> *yet the Saviour works mightily every day, drawing*
> *men to religion, persuading them to virtue, teaching*
> *them about immortality, quickening their thirst for*
> *heavenly things, revealing the knowledge of the Father,*
> *inspiring strength in face of death, manifesting Himself*
> *to each, and displacing the irreligion of idols.*

Athanasius concluded that the conversion of a sinner is "the work of One Who lives, not of one dead; and, more than that, it is the work of God."[1]

READ ACTS 9:1-9.

Would you say your conversion and testimony give a witness of the ascension and present work of Jesus?

Yes   No

Can people see a noticeable difference between who you are and the world or between who you are and who you once were?

Yes   No

When did the reality of who Jesus is transform your life? Though your conversion story may not seem as dramatic as Saul's, it's no less miraculous. Describe that experience.

How has Christ changed your life? Be specific.

Now let's look back at this week's study through the Apostles' Creed grid. You'll recall that this grid is provided as a filter you can use to examine and apply the doctrines outlined in this study.

1. SYMMETRY

The fact that Jesus ascended to heaven and sits at the right hand of the Father Almighty should give you confidence and a sense of holy discontentment—a refusal to settle for anything less than a life that glorifies the risen Lord.

2. CLARITY

You don't have to (and you can't) live the Christian life by your own strength. Your abilities have no effect on the righteousness of Christ and on your mission to be His witness. You live in His power. He's interceding on your behalf.

3. COMMUNITY

The living God, Jesus Christ, changed Saul's life. He can change anything in your life too. That also means He can change anybody around you, no matter how deeply entrenched in sin they may be. Because you can be sure that Jesus is alive and in control, you can have confidence that He's at work in and through you. You aren't yet what you'll be. He's not finished with you. He has made Himself known to you and is working through you as His witness.

4. COUNSEL

When you fall into temptation, don't give in to the paralysis of guilt and shame. You'll be surprised by how often your weaknesses can encourage and stir up the faith of your brothers and sisters in Christ. Allow God's radical work in your life—including your past sin and current struggles—to testify of the worthiness and power of Jesus Christ. Your Lord ever reigns at the right hand of the Father in heaven.

Thank God that Jesus is alive and in control, seated at His right hand with all authority. Pray for boldness to testify of His worthiness in your life.

1. St. Athanasius, *On the Incarnation*, trans. a religious of CSMV (Crestwood, NY: St. Vladimir's Seminary Press, 1944), 61–62.

Week Eight

I believe in God the Father Almighty,
Creator of heaven and earth,
And in Jesus Christ, His only Son, our Lord,
Who was conceived by the Holy Spirit;
born of the virgin Mary;
Suffered under Pontius Pilate;
was crucified, dead, and buried.
He descended to hell; the third day
He rose again from the dead;
He ascended to heaven and sits on the
right hand of the Father Almighty,
From whence He shall come to judge
the living and the dead.
I believe in the Holy Spirit,
The holy catholic church,
the communion of saints,
The forgiveness of sins,
The resurrection of the body,
and the life everlasting. Amen.

Group Study

START

FROM WHENCE HE SHALL COME TO JUDGE THE LIVING AND THE DEAD

Welcome everyone to week 8 of The Apostles' Creed.
Use this page to begin the group session.

Let's begin by taking a few minutes to review last week's study.

What was the most meaningful or challenging part of your personal study or family discipleship from "He ascended to heaven and sits on the right hand of the Father Almighty"? What did you learn or experience in a specific way this week?

Day 3 focused on the grid for understanding and applying the core doctrines summarized in the Apostles' Creed. Which of the four areas were most applicable this week and why? (Refer to p. 93 if needed.)

1. Symmetry: a balanced, robust understanding of biblical teaching
2. Clarity: a picture of who God truly is, not who we want Him to be
3. Community: an understanding of how to relate to one another as Christians
4. Counsel: an ability to speak biblical truth to ourselves and to others

Christians in our culture seem to forget or neglect the fact that Jesus not only rose from the dead and ascended to heaven but is also coming back. When kept in our hearts and minds, Jesus' return will transform our daily lives. He will return. When He returns, everyone will give an account for their lives and for their response to the gospel.

Read the Apostles' Creed aloud as a group before watching video session 8.

WATCH

*Use this viewer guide to follow along and
take notes as you watch video session 8.*

What's revealed in the return of Christ is His glory.

There's a day that all the nations and all the angels will sit around His glorious throne, and no one will dispute in that moment that He's King.

Jesus says that "I the Shepherd, I the Son of Man, I the King, that I will step in, and I'll separate the sheep from the goats."

The King who is the Judge, who is sitting in glory on His throne, associates Himself with the lowly.

1. SYMMETRY
We have a merciful Judge who is looking to us and giving us mercy.

We have a just Judge. He is right to punish sin.

You've been declared innocent because you stand in Christ and not on your own merits.

2. CLARITY
Christ takes no pleasure in the destruction of the wicked.

3. COMMUNITY
Not only all of the angels but all of the nations, all of the people surround the throne.

There should be a weightiness of mourning for brothers and sisters all throughout the world that are being persecuted. And there should be a rejoicing when the Lord does things all around the world.

4. COUNSEL
There's faithfulness in the practical obedience.

It's a call for us to be serious about the proclamation of the Kingdom.

 Video sessions available at lifeway.com/apostlescreed

DISCUSS

Discuss the video segment, using the following questions.

READ 2 TIMOTHY 4:1-2.

Why did this Scripture specify judgment as the reason for preaching, teaching, and making disciples of Jesus through the gospel?

Do you typically think of God as giving mercy or as rightly judging sin? What's the danger of thinking of Him as only just or only merciful?

Other than salvation, how have you specifically experienced God's mercy?

Are you more prone to want God to be just or merciful to other people?

How does the fact that Christ takes no pleasure in the destruction of the wicked affect the way you view others? How does it affect the way you view God?

What does it mean to mourn with Christians around the world who endure evil through persecution? How can we intentionally identify with the global church?

Why is it important to mourn and celebrate with believers, even those whom we'll never see in this life?

Knowing that judgment is a reality for all people, whom do you know who needs to hear the gospel of our merciful King? How will we hold one another accountable to share the urgent news of salvation by faith alone?

What's your primary observation about the teaching on "From whence He shall come to judge the living and the dead"?

What remaining thoughts or questions do you have?

Encourage members to complete the following personal studies before the next group session.

Family Discipleship

ENGAGE

The Apostles' Creed presents a great opportunity for families to consider the truths of the gospel together by utilizing the following framework for family discipleship: time, moments, and milestones.

☐ **TIME. Continue memorizing the Apostles' Creed as a family, being sure to add this phrase to your practice this week: "From whence He shall come to judge the living and the dead." Say the creed together before you pray at a meal or before you go to bed.**

☐ **MOMENTS. Be mindful of times when your family has to wait this week—in line at the store, for the mail to come, or in traffic. Waiting can be difficult. Point out the fact that there are good ways to wait and bad ways to wait. How do God's children wait for Jesus' return? What are God's children supposed to do as they wait? How does trusting God's promise that Jesus will return help us wait for Him with patient expectation?**

☐ **MILESTONES. What are some significant days coming up for your family that require preparation, waiting, and patience? How can you relate this kind of waiting to waiting for Christ's return?**

MEMORIZE

*Use this page to practice writing
the Apostles' Creed from memory.*

Personal Study

DAY 1

This week's portion of the creed closes out the part dealing with the person and work of Jesus. Having described Jesus' past and present ministry, this phrase describes His future work. These words direct our attention to Jesus' return. Remember what was said to the disciples on the Mount of Olives? Jesus' ascension was not only proof of His authority but also a promise of His return.

READ ACTS 1:6-11.

Why would Jesus' return be promised at the moment of His ascension?

What do Jesus' past ascension to heaven and His future return from heaven have to do with our present life on earth?

To understand the purpose of our lives and what it means to be witnesses (see Acts 1:8), it's important to consider the meaning and purpose of Jesus' coming.

READ HEBREWS 9:27-28.

With regard to believers, what was the purpose of Jesus' first coming?

What will be the purpose of His second coming?

Only a handful of disciples witnessed the Lord ascend to heaven. His birth was even less conspicuous. Even with a sky full of angels singing, only Mary, Joseph, and a few shepherds witnessed Jesus' coming into the world. However, His second coming will be unlike His first.

READ REVELATION 1:4-8.

What names and phrases are ascribed to Jesus? What do they emphasize?

Who will witness the second coming? How will those witnesses respond?

Rate how often you think about the fact that Jesus will return. Circle your answer.

1   2   3   4   5   6   7   8   9   10
Never   Constantly

Using the same scale, how would you rank your belief that Jesus will physically return to earth? Use a square for your answer.

Consider your answers to the two previous questions and compare the rankings marked by the circle and the square. What do your two scores reveal about your belief that Jesus could return any day—even today?

Why does it matter whether we believe Jesus will return?

Prayer

Heavenly Father, teach me to hope in the return of Jesus. Show me how to walk in wisdom as someone who expects to stand before Him, not to be punished but to give an account for my joyful obedience. Thank You that His return will mean the end of sin and suffering. In Jesus' name. Amen.

DAY 2

Although it hasn't happened yet, the second coming of Jesus is just as certain as His first coming. The question to ask yourself isn't whether He will return, because He will. The question to ask yourself isn't even a matter of when He will return, because we can't know. The only question you need to ask yourself is whether you're ready to stand before Him when He returns to judge the living and the dead.

READ MATTHEW 24:36-44.

The Bible teaches us that we can't know when Jesus will return and that we shouldn't waste time wondering but should always be ready.

Why did Jesus emphasize that nobody knows when He will return?

What would change if you knew Jesus would return this week?

I would ...

I would not ...

If you would change something because you knew the time of Jesus' return, what keeps you from making those changes now anyway?

Read the following parables and summarize key points in each.

Matthew 24:45-51

Matthew 25:1-13

Matthew 25:14-30

Matthew 25:31-46

Are the imagery and intensity of Jesus' stories surprising to you? What do they reveal about the nature of His return?

Based on the previous parables, what does it look like to eagerly anticipate Jesus' return?

Thank God for His justice and mercy. Ask Him for a spirit of anticipation
as you eagerly watch for His return and make the most of every
opportunity to share the gospel and to treat each day as if it could
be your last opportunity to show Christ's love to the world.

DAY 3

Most of the time we don't like to think about God's judgment. Unless we're seeking comfort in the fact that God will judge blatantly wicked people, we prefer to dwell on the God who "so loved the world, that he gave his only Son" (John 3:16). The grace of God through the sacrificial death of Jesus is indeed unique among major religions throughout history, but it's also because God is holy and good that He judges sin with incredible wrath.

The gospel is good news because without faith in Jesus, we would all rightfully receive the punishment we deserve for our sin. For those who belong to Christ, though, He has taken the punishment of death and God's wrath on Himself. But for those who haven't placed their faith in Jesus, refusing to bow their knee to Him as Lord, they'll receive the judgment they're due.

READ ROMANS 14:11-12.

How does giving an account for ourselves relate to bowing the knee and confessing Jesus as Lord?

People today debate religious beliefs or ignore Jesus altogether. They may view Him in various ways, some even positive, but the truth will be made clear in the end. There will be a day when all the nations and all the angels will sit around His glorious throne, and no one will dispute in that moment that He's King.

As we all give an account for every single thing we've done, there's no amount of good that will outweigh the bad—not for any of us. Justice will be served, and all sin will be accounted for. Ultimately, Jesus is the only reason we don't stand condemned in the sight of God. It was Jesus who completely took on our sin and paid the price in full, nailing our certificate of debt to His cross (see Col. 2:13-14).

READ REVELATION 20:11-15.

What thoughts and emotions do you have knowing that in the end justice will be served?

The incomparable beauty of the gospel is that the King, who's also the Judge, sitting in glory on His throne, associates Himself with the lowly and saves us.

Prayer

1. SYMMETRY

Take a moment to let the weight of eternal judgment sink in. You'll stand before God's throne to give an account for everything. That's a reality. Thank God that He's a just Judge who's right to punish sin and that you've been declared innocent because you stand in Christ and not on your own merits.

2. CLARITY

Ask God to break your heart over sin and to give you a burden to see people saved rather than judged. Keep in mind that Christ takes no pleasure in the destruction of the wicked (see Ezek. 33:11). He gave His only Son to die for us while we were still His enemies so that we could be made righteous in His sight (see Rom. 5:8).

3. COMMUNITY

Pray for the gospel to spread to every tribe, tongue, and nation. Pray for brothers and sisters in Christ throughout the world who are being persecuted.

4. COUNSEL

Pray for faithful endurance in the midst of all circumstances. Ask God to help you and your brothers and sisters in Christ keep your hope fixed on Jesus, knowing that in the end every knee will bow and every tongue confess that He is Lord (see Phil. 2:10-11).

Week Nine

I believe in God the Father Almighty,
    Creator of heaven and earth,
And in Jesus Christ, His only Son, our Lord,
Who was conceived by the Holy Spirit;
    born of the virgin Mary;
Suffered under Pontius Pilate;
    was crucified, dead, and buried.
He descended to hell; the third day
    He rose again from the dead;
He ascended to heaven and sits on the
    right hand of the Father Almighty,
From whence He shall come to judge
    the living and the dead.
I believe in the Holy Spirit,
The holy catholic church,
    the communion of saints,
The forgiveness of sins,
The resurrection of the body,
    and the life everlasting. Amen.

Group Study

START

I BELIEVE IN THE HOLY SPIRIT

*Welcome everyone to week 9 of The Apostles' Creed.
Use this page to begin the group session.*

Let's begin by taking a few minutes to review last week's study.

**What was the most meaningful or challenging part of your personal
study or family discipleship from "From whence He shall come to judge
the living and the dead"? What did you learn or experience in a specific
way this week?**

**Day 3 used our grid for understanding and applying each of the core
doctrines summarized in the Apostles' Creed as a guide for prayer.
Which of the four areas were most applicable this week and why?
(Refer to p. 105 if needed.)**

1. Symmetry: a balanced, robust understanding of biblical teaching
2. Clarity: a picture of who God truly is, not who we want Him to be
**3. Community: an understanding of how to relate to one another
   as Christians**
4. Counsel: an ability to speak biblical truth to ourselves and to others

The Apostles' Creed may seem to take a sudden turn in its train of thought this
week, but it backtracks a bit to fill in the gap between Jesus' ascension in the
past and His return in the future. What do we do in the meantime? While Christ
is seated at the right hand of God, the Holy Spirit is active and present in each
of His people. In fact, it's by the Spirit that we can understand and apply what
we'll study and discuss this week.

*Read the Apostles' Creed aloud as a group
before watching video session 9.*

WATCH

We were born with a desire to belong in a way that's beyond the belonging that's already naturally there by the grace of God.

We have this desire to belong, and yet nothing seems to satisfy that desire.

The more we try to fix our own lives, the more difficult and messy things get.

Being a son or daughter of God, being adopted into the family of God becomes an identity marker that nothing and no one can take from me.

This is what the Spirit of God does: ransoms us out of being spiritual orphans; pulls us into the household of faith; and gives us a marker of being known, loved, provided for, cared for, and pursued.

We're not obedient in order to be loved, but we are loved, and we understand love, and that love drives obedience.

The higher the love, the greater the capacity for self-sacrifice, for suffering, and ultimately for discipline.

The Holy Spirit informs and stirs up adoration that drives our obedience.

The people of God are prone to forget the faithfulness of God yesterday and simply complain about what they don't have today.

The peace that the world tries to bring isn't built in reality. The world can't keep its promises for us to actually walk in peace.

We can give ourselves over to that frantic, impossible pursuit of our best being enough, or we can melt and know we're not and know that He is able and rest in His ability over our inability.

The more we learn about Jesus, the more we remember the faithfulness of Jesus, the more we are able to walk in the peace that Jesus brings.

DISCUSS

Discuss the video segment, using the following questions.

READ ROMANS 8:14-15.

What confidence does it give you to have been adopted by the Father Almighty? What comfort do you experience in being able to call Him Abba?

Why did Matt say our natural desire to belong is a gift of God's grace?

In what ways, good or bad, do people seek to belong to something greater than themselves? How have you sought or experienced belonging?

How would you explain the difference between obedience driven by a desire to be lovable and obedience driven by knowing you're already loved? What does a lack of obedience to Jesus reveal?

READ JOHN 14:23-26.

According to Jesus, what's one of the primary roles of the Holy Spirit? What does this role look like in our daily lives?

How are knowledge, love, and obedience related?

What did Matt mean when he said it's blasphemous to minimize the Holy Spirit as merely the giver of spiritual gifts?

What's your primary observation about the teaching on "I believe in the Holy Spirit"?

What remaining thoughts or questions do you have?

Encourage members to complete the following personal studies before the next group session.

Family Discipleship

ENGAGE

The Apostles' Creed presents a great opportunity for families to consider the truths of the gospel together by utilizing the following framework for family discipleship: time, moments, and milestones.

- ☐ **TIME. Spend time as a family learning about the Holy Spirit. Look up the following passages and summarize what you learn from each one: John 14:25-26; 16:7-8,13; Acts 1:8; 4:31; and Romans 8:26-27. Continue memorizing the Apostles' Creed as a family, adding the phrase "I believe in the Holy Spirit." Practice saying the creed together whenever you pray as a family.**

- ☐ **MOMENTS. The Holy Spirit helps God's children. Parents, look for opportunities to joyfully help your children this week. Point out that you're able to help them because you are stronger, are smarter, have experienced more of life, have more authority, and so on. Emphasize that it delights you to help them because you love them, just as the Holy Spirit delights to help God's children know and obey Him. We can and should ask for the Spirit's help and find ways to help one another.**

- ☐ **MILESTONES. Make your children's birthdays an opportunity to point out ways the Holy Spirit has uniquely gifted them as believers to be part of the body of Christ and to help build up the body. Affirm how God made them: spiritual gifts, talents, interests, strengths, character traits, and so on. Challenge your children to use and invest their gifts for God's glory and the good of others.**

MEMORIZE

*Use this page to practice writing
the Apostles' Creed from memory.*

Personal Study

DAY 1

Christians believe God is a Trinity. We've already seen that God has eternally existed as one essence and three distinct persons: God the Father, God the Son, and God the Holy Spirit. Each of the three persons of the Godhead is fully God, yet there's one God. The Apostles' Creed affirms the trinitarian formula when it affirms belief in the Holy Spirit.

The following passage describes each person of the Trinity.

READ JOHN 16:7-15.

Why did Jesus tell His disciples that it's to their advantage for Him to go away—ascend to heaven—and for them to have the Spirit instead?

How did Jesus refer to the Holy Spirit? What do the names suggest?

According to Jesus, what would the Spirit do? Be specific.

Sometimes people speak of the Holy Spirit in impersonal terms. In contrast, Jesus referred to the Spirit as *He, Helper,* and *Guide*. The Spirit is never an *it*.

Why is it essential that we speak of the Holy Spirit in personal terms?

The Bible testifies that no one can know Christ except by the Holy Spirit. Therefore, the Spirit is known as the One who gives life (see John 6:63).

READ JOHN 3:1-8.

We get the phrase *born-again Christian* from Jesus' words in John 3:3. To be a part of God's eternal family, to live forever in His heavenly kingdom, we must be born again. The Greek word *anōthen,* translated here as "again," can also be translated as "from above." In other words, verses 3 and 5 are clear that spiritual life requires spiritual birth.

Have you been born again, born from above, born of the Holy Spirit? How do you know you've received the gift of life from the Spirit?

READ EPHESIANS 1:3-10.

When the Father gives the Holy Spirit to you, you also receive all of Christ's benefits of sonship. Your justification, sanctification, adoption, and glorification come to you through your union with Christ, which is given only by the Spirit. Therefore, all of salvation, from beginning to end, is a gift from God the Father, accomplished by God the Son, and given through God the Holy Spirit.

How does this trinitarian conception of salvation encourage you to believe that all of salvation is yours through the gift of the Spirit?

Prayer

Father, thank You for drawing me by Your Holy Spirit to your beautiful Son. The indwelling presence of the Spirit gives me more joy and peace than anything this world could provide. Please help me walk in accordance with the Spirit and not the flesh. Thank You for the gift of knowing You through Your Holy Spirit. Amen.

DAY 2

The Holy Spirit is specifically mentioned in the Apostles' Creed because the Bible teaches that the Spirit isn't the Father, nor is He the Son, yet He's fully God. Because the Spirit is fully God and God is a personal God, the Spirit has personal attributes, and He acts personally.

READ JOHN 14:26 AND 1 JOHN 2:18-27.

According to these two texts, what does the Holy Spirit teach us?

It's vital for believers to be able to discern spiritual truth from lies. One job of the Holy Spirit is to help us read and understand the Bible. This doctrine is called illumination. Illumination means God must enlighten the human mind in order for us to understand the things of God. The Spirit renews our minds and restores our senses by revealing spiritual truth to us.

READ 1 CORINTHIANS 2:10-16.

What does verse 14 say about a person's natural ability to comprehend spiritual truth?

Is this passage encouraging, discouraging, or both? Explain your answer.

What does it mean to read the Bible with the mind of Christ?

While the Holy Spirit works in accordance with the Father and the Son to bring about salvation in the lives of believers, the Spirit also enables us to live as Christians by His power.

READ GALATIANS 5:16-24.

According to Paul, all virtue is born of the Holy Spirit, and all vice is born of the flesh.

From which failings of the flesh do you seek the Spirit's help to be free?

How do you seek the Holy Spirit's power in resisting fleshly vice?

What specific fruit of the Spirit have you noticed most evidently in your life since you've known Christ?

What fruit of the Spirit, through God's regenerative and preserving mercy, would you like to exhibit more in your life?

Prayer

Holy, triune God, I give You all honor and praise. Have mercy on me. Give me a humble heart. Holy Spirit, help me never lose sight of the person and work of Jesus Christ. Illumine and enlighten my mind to spiritual things. Reveal to me the beautiful truth of Scripture. Lead me out of darkness and into the way of Christ. Make me a faithful, righteous person known by faith, hope, and love. Spirit of God, never let me depart from the truth that You teach me in Christ. Preserve me forever in my love for the Savior. I ask these things in the name of Jesus Christ, my Lord and King. Amen.

DAY 3

The Spirit of God literally changes everything about your life. He ransoms you, saving you from being a spiritual orphan; bringing you into the household of faith; and marking you as a son or a daughter of God who's known, loved, provided for, cared for, and pursued. Being adopted into the family of God is an identity marker that nothing and no one can take from you. Through faith in the Son, by the grace of the Father, you're a Spirit-filled member of His family.

READ JOHN 15:26 AND ACTS 2:1-4.

The Father and the Son sent the Holy Spirit to the church in one of the most climactic events in salvation history—Pentecost. The Spirit was poured out on the church as a gift from the Father and the Son. The triune God created a new Spirit-born people—the church—characterized by the indwelling presence of the Holy Spirit.

In what way is the gift of the Holy Spirit greater than any other gift we could receive, even from God?

The Holy Spirit indwells believers and uniquely gives them and the church the gift of discerning and receiving the truth about God (see 1 John 1:1-3; 4:6) and rejecting false teaching (see 4:1). The Spirit unites believers and enables us to abide in Christ. The Spirit also fills us and gives us Christlike character that's powerfully different from the way we once lived according to the flesh (see Gal. 5:16-26; Col. 3:1-17).

Read 2 Timothy 1:7. In what ways is fear the opposite of power, love, and self-control?

In what areas of your life can the Holy Spirit help you live with greater power, love, and self-control?

The Holy Spirit is now the presence of Christ everywhere, available to all believers at any given moment. Now, with the Holy Spirit, humans are turned into proper vessels for cosmic renewal. Let this awesome reality sink in as you use the four areas of our theological grid to guide your time of reflection and prayer.

1. SYMMETRY

How does the Holy Spirit give believers a robust understanding of the Bible?

2. CLARITY

Why would you have an incomplete understanding of who God is without a right belief in the Holy Spirit? Who is the Holy Spirit?

3. COMMUNITY

How does the Holy Spirit provide unity among fellow believers in Christ?

4. COUNSEL

What truth has the Holy Spirit impressed on you, illuminating your mind as you've studied this week's lessons?

How can you rely on the Holy Spirit when you give and receive counsel from other brothers and sisters in Christ?

Prayer

Thank God for the life-changing gift of His Spirit. Take time listening to the Spirit in prayer. Be still and quiet as you ask the Spirit for discernment to be aware of His guidance and spiritual ears and eyes to recognize what He reveals to you.

Week Ten

I believe in God the Father Almighty,
    Creator of heaven and earth,
And in Jesus Christ, His only Son, our Lord,
Who was conceived by the Holy Spirit;
    born of the virgin Mary;
Suffered under Pontius Pilate;
    was crucified, dead, and buried.
He descended to hell; the third day
    He rose again from the dead;
He ascended to heaven and sits on the
    right hand of the Father Almighty,
From whence He shall come to judge
    the living and the dead.
I believe in the Holy Spirit,
The holy catholic church,
    the communion of saints,
The forgiveness of sins,
The resurrection of the body,
    and the life everlasting. Amen.

Group Study

START

THE HOLY CATHOLIC CHURCH, THE COMMUNION OF SAINTS

Welcome everyone to week 10 of The Apostles' Creed. Use this page to begin the group session.

Let's begin by taking a few minutes to review last week's study.

What was the most meaningful or challenging part of your personal study or family discipleship from "I believe in the Holy Spirit"? What did you learn or experience in a specific way this week?

Day 3 focused on the grid for understanding and applying the core doctrines summarized in the Apostles' Creed. Which of the four areas were most applicable this week and why? (Refer to p. 117 if needed.)

1. Symmetry: a balanced, robust understanding of biblical teaching

2. Clarity: a picture of who God truly is, not who we want Him to be

3. Community: an understanding of how to relate to one another as Christians

4. Counsel: an ability to speak biblical truth to ourselves and to others

The Holy Spirit isn't aimlessly floating through the world. He indwells and empowers the church—the community of God's people. As brothers and sisters in Christ, we're united by faith in the Son and adopted by the Father Almighty. The Apostles' Creed gives a unified voice to Christians around the world and throughout history. We're a global family waiting for a heavenly home.

Read the Apostles' Creed aloud as a group before watching video session 10.

WATCH

Because we've been made in the image of God, we are more valuable than
the rest of the creative order.

Everyone has God as their Creator, but not everyone has God as their Father.

The biblical worldview for your life and mine is that we might be in right relationship
with God and one another.

When the Apostles' Creed says "the holy catholic church," it's referencing all
Christians everywhere over all time as a part of our family, a part of something
we belong to.

It's God's good design that we would belong to a local church, not that we would
go to one. That's different than belonging.

1. SYMMETRY
If you know everyone, you don't know anyone.

God's call on our lives is deep, rich friendships that are rooted and established
in how He has called us to Himself.

2. CLARITY
God has called you to Himself. In calling you to Himself, He has called you
to others, both to be a blessing and to receive the blessing of others.

3. COMMUNITY
I cannot do it all. I cannot have it all.

4. COUNSEL
The Christian is open to the counsel of others.

The tangible presence of God is most often revealed in living among the communion
of the saints.

DISCUSS

Discuss the video segment, using the following questions.

Matt began by asking two questions: How are you living out the one anothers in Scripture? What practical steps are you taking to make room for meaningful relationships, including your church and small group? How would you answer these questions?

How would you explain the difference between going to and belonging to a local church? Would you say you go to or belong to your church? How long have you belonged to your church? What has been the greatest blessing of being part of that community?

Why is it equally important to be a blessing and to receive blessings?

How often do you think about being called by God into relationships with other Christians? How does this calling shape your view of your church?

Do the statements "I can't do it all; I can't have it all" convict or encourage you? In what ways do you try to either do it all or have it all?

READ PROVERBS 11:14.

When have you been blessed by the counsel of other Christians? In what ways has God convicted, encouraged, or taught you through conversations and relationships with other people in this group?

What's your primary observation about the teaching on "The holy catholic church, the communion of saints"?

What remaining thoughts or questions do you have?

Encourage members to complete the following personal studies before the next group session.

Family Discipleship

ENGAGE

The Apostles' Creed presents a great opportunity for families to consider the truths of the gospel together by utilizing the following framework for family discipleship: time, moments, and milestones.

☐ **TIME. Set aside time to read and discuss Acts 2:42-47. This passage tells us what life was like for the early church—the first Christians. What did they spend their time doing? What actions marked their gathering and the way they related to one another? How do those things compare to church practice today? Continue memorizing the Apostles' Creed as a family. Practice it together before you pray at a meal or before you go to bed.**

☐ **MOMENTS. The church is a people, not a place. Throughout the week point out all the places where you see the church—not when you drive by the church building but where you see believers: small group, ministry opportunities, worship service, friends at dinner, and so on.**

☐ **MILESTONES. Consider having a conversation with your kids about the importance of church membership. As a part of the conversation, encourage them to look forward to a day when they'll have the opportunity to join a church as members. As a family, commit to celebrate those times as milestones when they occur.**

MEMORIZE

Use this page to practice writing the Apostles' Creed from memory.

Personal Study

DAY 1

At this point the Apostles' Creed turns its attention from the nature of God and the gospel to the people who are created as a result of the gospel—the church. After Jesus ascended to the Father, the Father and the Son sent the Holy Spirit, an event that's described in Acts 2. The day of Pentecost was the birth of the church, a community that was brought into existence by the life-giving Spirit of Christ.

In week 7 you read the end of Peter's first sermon (see vv. 32-38). The response to his message resulted in the baptism of over three thousand people and the beginning of the church (see v. 41).

READ ACTS 2:42-47.

What characteristics defined the church? List them here.

What words described the experiences of the church? List them here.

READ EPHESIANS 4:4-7.

In this passage what distinct roles do the three persons of the Trinity (Father, Son, and Spirit) play in the formation of the church?

Ephesians focuses our attention on what we have in common: one church and one God.

What specific things do Christians share in common that unite us?

Who's a part of your gospel-centered community (the communion of saints)? Record the names of the people in your small group or other close friends in your local church.

Whom do you know who isn't connected to a church or who attends church but isn't connected to a small group or another meaningful form of gospel-centered community? Commit to invite them to join you or encourage them to connect with a local church in their area.

While it may seem popular or culturally acceptable today to believe you can be a Christian without being committed to a local church, that idea is absolutely foreign to biblical Christianity, both today and throughout church history. Equally unfounded is the attempt to say you can belong to the universal church (the meaning of *catholic* in the creed) but not to a local church.

READ HEBREWS 10:24-25.

According to these verses, what's one major purpose of meeting regularly?

Record the regular schedule of times you meet with your church, small group, Bible study, discipleship group, or other ministry activities.

Father, I thank You that You've established Your church on the foundation of Your sovereign authority. You've called to Yourself a people who can find joy and hope in worshiping You. Lord, make me restless until I find my rest in You. Help me see the church as holy because that's what You've made it. Help me see the church as one because You're one. Help me see the church as a beautiful communion You've called me to participate in and join. In Jesus' name I pray. Amen.

DAY 2

Humans are relational creatures. We're made for community. Before sin entered the world, the first thing in all creation that God deemed "not good" was "that the man should be alone" (see Gen. 2:18). After all, we're created in the image of a triune God: Father, Son, and Spirit (see 1:26-27). God enjoys community within Himself.

Relationships are a simple concept, but particular dynamics can be unique, so Scripture uses various metaphors to describe the sacred communal relationship known as the church.

Read the following Scriptures, identify the image used in each, and summarize a way it's helpful in understanding the church.

READ EPHESIANS 2:19-22.

Image describing the church:

How it helps you understand the church:

READ EPHESIANS 5:22-32.

Image describing the church:

How it helps you understand the church:

One defining characteristic of a marriage relationship is that a husband and a wife are one flesh, echoing God's blessing on Adam and Eve (see Gen. 2:24). Similarly, the church is united with Christ and is made one by the Holy Spirit (see 1 Cor. 6:17).

READ COLOSSIANS 1:15-20.

Image describing the church:

How it helps you understand the church:

READ 1 CORINTHIANS 12:12-26.

Image describing the church:

How it helps you understand the church:

This passage beautifully describes the diverse members of the body of Christ and the diverse spiritual gifts that make up one body. Be sure to reread verses 22-26. There's no gift that God doesn't honor.

How do you use your gifts, skills, and experiences to serve the church?

To You, Father, and to the Son and to the Holy Spirit are due all honor, glory, and worship. I thank You, Father, for transferring me from the dominion of darkness into the kingdom of Your Son, who reigns as Head over His body, the church. Your church desires to be one as You are one. Shape Your church into the likeness of Christ. Your church, the communion of saints in which You've placed us, is holy and set apart, not because of its merit but because You've called Your people into fellowship. By your mercy allow my local church to extend the gospel to its neighbors and the nations for the sake of Christ's kingdom. I pray in the name of my Lord Jesus. Amen.

DAY 3

Three key words in this week's section of the Apostles' Creed should be reemphasized for clarity: *catholic, saints,* and *communion.*

When the Apostles' Creed says "the holy catholic church," it's referring to the body of Christ to which all Christians everywhere over all time belong. The word *catholic* is translated from a Greek word, *katholikos,* that means "according to the whole, or universal." In saying the church is catholic, we're affirming that all Christians everywhere are included in the communion of the saints. Therefore, the term *catholic* isn't a reference to a specific denomination or to what we now know as the Roman Catholic Church. All Spirit-indwelled, gospel-believing, Jesus-exalting Christians are part of the holy catholic church.

Second, when the Apostles' Creed says "saints," it's another reference to all believers. This isn't a reference to a position or status in a church reserved for a few exceptional individuals. All 60 times the New Testament uses the term, it indicates all Christians. The Greek word *hagios* literally means "holy ones." In Christ we've been made holy. The saints gather and commune as the church.

Finally, when the Apostles' Creed says "communion," it's referring to the communal gathering of the saints—Christians—as the church.

Essentially, the phrase "The holy catholic church, the communion of saints" is purposely redundant, emphasizing the totality and inclusivity of all believers in the body of Christ.

READ 1 PETER 2:4-10.

List the words used in this passage to describe the value, identity, and purpose of the church—the communion of all saints.

Value:

Identity:

Purpose:

Because we've been made in the image of God, we're more valuable than the rest of the created order. God desires to commune with us as His people. The tangible presence of God is most often revealed in the communion of saints. It's God's good design that we *belong* to a local church, not that we *go* to one. There's an important difference. God has invited you into something greater—new relationships, new community, and new life as His church.

Prayer

1. SYMMETRY

Thank God for your church and for creating you for meaningful relationships.

2. CLARITY

Ask God to draw you closer to Him as you draw closer to His people.

3. COMMUNITY

Pray for people in your small group by name, including any specific requests. Take a minute to connect with at least one other person to ask how you can pray for him or her.

4. COUNSEL

Seek out a trusted member of your small group or a church leader and openly share about your life, asking that person to pray for you.

Week Eleven

I believe in God the Father Almighty,
    Creator of heaven and earth,
And in Jesus Christ, His only Son, our Lord,
Who was conceived by the Holy Spirit;
    born of the virgin Mary;
Suffered under Pontius Pilate;
    was crucified, dead, and buried.
He descended to hell; the third day
    He rose again from the dead;
He ascended to heaven and sits on the
    right hand of the Father Almighty,
From whence He shall come to judge
    the living and the dead.
I believe in the Holy Spirit,
The holy catholic church,
    the communion of saints,
The forgiveness of sins,
The resurrection of the body,
    and the life everlasting. Amen.

Group Study

START

THE FORGIVENESS OF SINS

*Welcome everyone to week 11 of The Apostles' Creed.
Use this page to begin the group session.*

Let's begin by taking a few minutes to review last week's study.

What was the most meaningful or challenging part of your personal study or family discipleship from "The holy catholic church, the communion of saints"? What did you learn or experience in a specific way this week?

For the final time day 3 used our grid for understanding and applying each of the core doctrines summarized in the Apostles' Creed as a guide for prayer. Which of the four areas were most applicable this week and why? (Refer to p. 129 if needed.)

1. Symmetry: a balanced, robust understanding of biblical teaching
2. Clarity: a picture of who God truly is, not who we want Him to be
3. Community: an understanding of how to relate to one another as Christians
4. Counsel: an ability to speak biblical truth to ourselves and to others

Although we don't often think about ourselves as saints, we should. God has set us apart as a holy people, the church. We're holy, but we aren't yet perfect in our sanctification. The Christian life is one of forgiveness. We're justified through faith in Christ, once and for all. However, sanctification is an ongoing ethic of confession and repentance. We must continually be forgiven of our sins, and we must continually forgive those who sin against us.

*Read the Apostles' Creed aloud as a group
before watching video session 11.*

WATCH

*Use this viewer guide to follow along and
take notes as you watch video session 11.*

GOD'S FORGIVENESS IN THE OLD TESTAMENT

1. God forgives.
2. God's people are the stage upon which the forgiveness of God is made visible.

Forgiveness helps us understand and see most clearly who God is.

WHAT GOD FORGIVES US OF

1. Iniquity is a premeditated choice that carries with it some continuing disregard
   for repentance.
2. Transgression is presumptuous sin, arrogant sin. This is to choose to willfully disobey.
3. Sin is to miss the mark.

Sin carries with it collateral damage. When you sin against God, you also sin
against others.

The people of God are never more authentic than when they ask for forgiveness
and forgive others.

1. SYMMETRY

You must embrace and believe that you can be forgiven.

2. CLARITY

There is no iniquity, transgression, or sin that is more powerful than the forgiveness of God in Christ. Forgiveness of others is a command.

3. COMMUNITY

If you and I want to walk in the communion of saints, then confession of sins
is an ongoing ethic of what happens.

4. COUNSEL

If I can be mindful of how God's forgiven me, then I am able to extend forgiveness
to others.

God loves to wipe away debts and break all the rules of a punishment-obsessed world.

DISCUSS

Discuss the video segment, using the following questions.

READ LUKE 15:20-24.

In what ways do you relate to the prodigal son?

Even if we're truly forgiven, what damage is done in our lives when we don't embrace and believe the fact that we can be forgiven of our sins?

How does unconfessed sin affect Christian community? When have your relationships suffered due either to unconfessed sin or to the inability to believe you were truly forgiven?

When have you forgiven someone you know you wouldn't have been able to forgive if not for God's work in your heart?

How did Matt distinguish among iniquity, transgression, and sin? What are examples of each? How are the definitions helpful in understanding forgiveness?

What's your primary observation about the teaching on "The forgiveness of sins"?

What remaining thoughts or questions do you have?

Encourage members to complete the following personal studies before the next group session.

Family Discipleship

ENGAGE

The Apostles' Creed presents a great opportunity for families to consider the truths of the gospel together by utilizing the following framework for family discipleship: time, moments, and milestones.

- ☐ **TIME.** During your family discipleship time compose a definition of the word *forgiveness*. **Read Colossians 1:13-14 and emphasize that believers are forgiven because of Jesus' death and resurrection. Continue memorizing the Apostles' Creed as a family. Practice it together before you pray at a meal or before you go to bed.**

- ☐ **MOMENTS. There will likely be many opportunities in your family this week to talk about forgiveness. Explain that God forgives His children because of Jesus. As you practice both extending and receiving forgiveness, point your children to the fact that, ultimately, we need forgiveness from God first before we seek forgiveness from others.**

- ☐ **MILESTONES. In an age-appropriate way, share your testimony with your kids. Tell them how and from what God saved you and when you received the forgiveness of your sin by faith in Jesus. Develop a plan to mark and celebrate the salvation of your kids.**

MEMORIZE

*Use this page to practice writing
the Apostles' Creed from memory.*

Personal Study

DAY 1

In the first two chapters of the Bible, we see the world as God intends. Beauty, communion, truth, love, happiness, and work mark the first few pages of our Bible in a way that's utterly stunning. However, by Genesis 3 sin begins its destructive path into the world, leaving all creation fractured and broken.

READ GENESIS 3.

Identify key points in this text and the general principles behind them.

God's law:
Example: The command not to eat from the tree revealed God's wisdom and goodness. He desires what's best for us. We trust Him even if we don't understand.

Temptation and sin:

Judgment:

Grace:

What effects of Adam and Eve's sin extend beyond their own personal consequences? What do these effects reveal about the nature of sin?

What do you learn about God's forgiveness in this account of the first sin?

All who are Adam's children (all humanity) have been diagnosed with the disease of sin. All of us are rotten branches because we were born from a rotten root. Theologically, this concept is known as the doctrine of original sin (see Ps. 51:5; Rom. 5:12-21; 1 Cor. 15:21-22). For many people, this doctrine is scandalous because they think they shouldn't be held responsible for Adam's sin.

Why are we held responsible for Adam's sin? In what way were we in the garden with him?

READ ROMANS 3:10-18.

How does the description of humanity's sinful condition differ from the world's perspective on humanity and on what's acceptable or excusable?

READ HEBREWS 8:12.

It can be tempting for us to believe the lie that we're so stained by sin that we can't be made clean. Despite the seriousness of our sin, God's mercy triumphs, and He doesn't even recall our sins He has forgiven.

Do you struggle to believe every sin of every kind can be forgiven? What makes any sin unique and less forgivable in your mind?

READ LUKE 7:36-50.

This is the story of all who believe. Meditate on Jesus' declaration in verse 48. Consider the way Jesus handled sin in every encounter during His public ministry on earth. You won't find any exclusion from God's forgiveness.

Read this prayer aloud: "Most merciful God, we confess that we have sinned against thee in thought, word, and deed, by what we have done, and by what we have left undone. We have not loved thee with our whole heart; we have not loved our neighbors as ourselves. We are truly sorry and we humbly repent. For the sake of thy Son Jesus Christ, have mercy on us and forgive us; that we may delight in thy will, and walk in thy ways, to the glory of thy Name. Amen."[1]

1. *The Book of Common Prayer* (New York: Church Publishing Inc., 2001), 320.

DAY 2

Too often we make sin an abstract idea instead of a deadly reality. Other times we limit sin to heinous acts of immorality. Compared to those acts, what we think, say, or do doesn't seem so bad. After all, nobody's perfect, right?

What are some words people use to soften the severity of sin?

J. I. Packer helpfully summarized the scope of our sin when he said:

It is lawlessness in relation to God as lawgiver, rebellion in relation to God as rightful ruler, missing the mark in relation to God as our designer, guilt in relation to God as judge, and uncleanness in relation to God as the Holy One. Sin is a perversity touching each one of us at every point in our lives.[1]

Which one of Packer's descriptions is most helpful to you in understanding the nature of sin?

What's the danger of not taking sin seriously?

Thomas Watson, an English Puritan, once said, "Till sin be bitter, Christ will not be sweet."[2] For some of us, sin isn't bitter. It has actually become common, trivial, or even a matter of preference. But we can't fully appreciate the depths of God's forgiveness if we don't understand the depths of our sin.

READ ROMANS 1:18-25.

Describe the severe nature of sin, according to this passage.

READ PSALM 130.

When was the last time you cried out for God's mercy, recognizing the severity of sin in your life?

READ 1 JOHN 1:5-9.

Bringing sin into the light is painful and scary, but it's also restorative and freeing.

To what truth about God are we testifying when we confess our sins not only to God but also to one another?

Providing forgiveness for our sins is at the heart of what God is doing in the world through the person and work of Christ. All other aspects of salvation (reconciliation, justification, sanctification, and redemption) find their hope in the simple idea of forgiveness.

Prayer

Lord, I confess that You're faithful even when I'm faithless. I acknowledge that You found me when I was dead in my trespasses and sins. Thank You for not forsaking me. Like the psalmist, "I know my transgressions, and my sin is ever before me. Against you, you only, have I sinned and done what is evil in your sight" (Ps. 51:3-4). I have broken Your law; I was born a rebel who rejected Your love. But thanks be to God, You don't count my iniquities: "With you there is forgiveness, that you may be feared" (Ps. 130:4). You're the God who forgives sinners. Praise be the name of my great God! Amen.

1. J. I. Packer, *Growing in Christ* (Wheaton, IL: Crossway, 1994), 79.
2. Thomas Watson, "The Doctrine of Repentance," The-Highway.com [online, cited 6 December 2016]. Available from the Internet: the-highway.com/repentance_Watson.html.

DAY 3

Describing his own sin, Augustine said, "My sin was that I looked for pleasure, beauty, and truth not in [God] but in myself and his other creatures. That search led me instead to pain, confusion, and error."[1]

Do you resonate with Augustine's understanding of sin? In what ways do you look for good things in the wrong places? What's the result?

READ 1 JOHN 1:5-10.

God's people are the stage on which His forgiveness is made visible. The people of God are never more authentic than when they ask for forgiveness and forgive others.

1. SYMMETRY

To experience freedom from your sin, you must admit your sin and believe you can be forgiven.

Do you struggle with admitting your sin, even to yourself?

Identify at least one recurring sin that you continually struggle with.

Identify a sin that has recently surprised you, perhaps something that you hadn't struggled with in a long time or had never dealt with before.

2. CLARITY

There's no iniquity, transgression, or sin that's more powerful than the forgiveness of God in Christ. God can—and will—forgive any confessed sin of which you repent. Sin can do real damage, however, when you don't repent, believing it's not worth dealing with. First John makes clear that knowingly walking in sin isn't compatible with following Jesus. It destroys fellowship with God and the church.

3. COMMUNITY

If you want to walk in the communion of the saints, confession of sins is an ongoing ethic you must constantly practice.

Identify someone to whom you'll confess specific sin, asking for accountability to walk in forgiveness and holiness.

Whom do you need to ask for forgiveness? If you've sinned against someone else or if your sins have affected other people, confess your sins to those people and ask for their forgiveness.

4. COUNSEL

READ MATTHEW 6:14-15 AND 1 JOHN 4:19.

Whom do you need to forgive?

What will you do to keep God's forgiveness of you in the forefront of your mind so that you can extend forgiveness to others?

Thank God that He first loved you, making forgiveness and freedom in Christ possible. Confess your sins to Him and ask for humility and courage to confess sins to others and to ask for the forgiveness of people you've sinned against. Pray that you'll trust the goodness of God's Word, believing confession brings forgiveness and healing.

1. Augustine, as quoted in Richard H. Schmidt, *God Seekers: 20 Centuries of Christian Spiritualities* (Grand Rapids, MI: Eerdmans, 2008), 54.

Week Twelve

I believe in God the Father Almighty,
    Creator of heaven and earth,
And in Jesus Christ, His only Son, our Lord,
Who was conceived by the Holy Spirit;
    born of the virgin Mary;
Suffered under Pontius Pilate;
    was crucified, dead, and buried.
He descended to hell; the third day
    He rose again from the dead;
He ascended to heaven and sits on the
    right hand of the Father Almighty,
From whence He shall come to judge
    the living and the dead.
I believe in the Holy Spirit,
The holy catholic church,
    the communion of saints,
The forgiveness of sins,
The resurrection of the body,
    and the life everlasting. Amen.

Group Study

START

THE RESURRECTION OF THE BODY, AND THE LIFE EVERLASTING. AMEN.

Welcome everyone to week 12 of The Apostles' Creed.
Use this page to begin the group session.

Let's begin by taking a few minutes to review last week's study.

What was the most meaningful or challenging part of your personal study or family discipleship from "The forgiveness of sins"? What did you learn or experience in a specific way this week?

Day 3 focused on the grid for understanding and applying the core doctrines summarized in the Apostles' Creed. Which of the four areas were most applicable this week and why? (Refer to pp. 140–41 if needed.)

1. Symmetry: a balanced, robust understanding of biblical teaching
2. Clarity: a picture of who God truly is, not who we want Him to be
3. Community: an understanding of how to relate to one another as Christians
4. Counsel: an ability to speak biblical truth to ourselves and to others

Our lives and our hope aren't ultimately satisfied with the forgiveness of sins, as glorious as that is. The creed doesn't stop there, and the Bible doesn't stop there. Forgiveness is a vital step along the way to even greater joy. In our final session we'll focus on the promise of resurrection and eternal life.

Recite from memory or read the Apostles' Creed aloud as a group before watching video session 12.

WATCH

*Use this viewer guide to follow along and
take notes as you watch video session 12.*

It's what you're hoping for and what you hope in that drives everything about
how you're living your life.

Misplaced hope is catastrophic.

You will become a slave to your ultimate hope.

"The resurrection of the body, and life everlasting"—this phrase is the foundation
of Christian hope, Christian courage, and the ordering of the Christian life.

When we're talking about Christian hope in the bodily resurrection, we're talking
about resurrection and not resuscitation.

It's going to be a physical resurrection. This is the base of Christian hope.
This is the base of Christian courage. I've got eternity.

I am physically resurrected in bodily form to life everlasting.

1. SYMMETRY
Some of us are putting undue hope on things that can't deliver.

2. CLARITY
There's a physical, bodily resurrection.

3. COMMUNITY
There's an awareness that drives us to kindness and compassion because
we know that all of us are eternal beings.

4. COUNSEL
Since we are eternal creatures, then we take seriously the eternality of our souls.

The engine that beings to drive the activity of your life is now no longer a misplaced
hope but a rightly placed ultimate hope in what Christ has done for us in the cross.

DISCUSS

Discuss the video segment, using the following questions.

Matt taught at length on the importance of our hope as believers. Which of his closing questions or the viewer-guide statements about hope was most thought-provoking for you and why?

READ 1 CORINTHIANS 15:54-57.

How do resurrection and eternal life reorient our hope and our perspective on the sting of death and life's disappointments?

Why is it significant that God resurrects our bodies and restores creation rather than making something entirely different?

The creed, like the Bible, begins with God as Creator and concludes with eternal life in a resurrected state. How do these two points relate to each other? Why are these important starting and ending points for what we believe?

What was most helpful to you in the points of symmetry, clarity, community, and counsel? Why?

What's your primary observation about the teaching on "The resurrection of the body, and the life everlasting"?

What are some key truths you've learned from this study of the Apostles' Creed? How has your understanding of doctrine in general or of a specific doctrine changed? How would you explain to someone what you've learned in this study?

Did anyone memorize the creed? Was it a helpful exercise? Do you plan to continue the discipline of memorization? If so, what Scriptures? Did anyone use the family-discipleship guides? How beneficial was that experience? Has it helped established a rhythm for family worship?

Encourage members to complete the final personal studies to conclude The Apostles' Creed.

Family Discipleship

ENGAGE

The Apostles' Creed presents a great opportunity for families to consider the truths of the gospel together by utilizing the following framework for family discipleship: time, moments, and milestones.

- ☐ **TIME. Set aside time this week to examine and discuss ways you or others see the world. Then read Revelation 21:1-8. What will life be like when Jesus returns? What are the differences between our world now and the new heaven and the new earth? Continue memorizing the Apostles' Creed as a family. Practice it together before you pray at a meal or before you go to bed.**

- ☐ **MOMENTS. Use everyday experiences as opportunities to identify ways this world is broken and imperfect. Point out our yearning for the Lord to make all things new.**

- ☐ **MILESTONES. The next time a loved one, family friend, or neighbor passes away, consider taking the opportunity to share the good news of the resurrection of the dead with your children. They'll be confronted by the reality of death for the rest of their lives, just as you've been. Make sure when they think about death, they're reminded that people who are in Christ will one day be raised with Him with new bodies that are incorruptible and imperishable. In the face of death, teach your children to grieve but not like those without resurrection hope (see 1 Thess. 4:13).**

MEMORIZE

*Use this page to practice writing
the Apostles' Creed from memory.*

Personal Study

DAY 1

Every religious tradition, every culture, every family, and every individual has some concept of hope. Of course, the object of hope can differ quite significantly from person to person or from culture to culture, but everyone is hoping for something. For example, one of the main forms of hope that has captured the minds and imaginations of our culture is the hope of progress. The promise of progress tells us things are constantly getting better; culture is making strides toward greater freedom, greater liberty, better health, greater medical advances, fewer problems, and more enjoyment. But we know that no matter what we achieve, things don't get any better. We may improve our quality of life—maybe—but sin, brokenness, and death are still inescapable. We can't repair the fracture in our lives or in the world around us.

Christians, however, have real hope. As we've already studied, we're not immune to problems, and we're not perfect. We don't have a forced smile that's oblivious to the pain and suffering in life. We don't think a believe-it-to-achieve-it positivity is going to make everything work out in the end. We know something much, much better. Something true. Something real. We know the end of the story, and death isn't the end.

READ ISAIAH 25:6-9.

Describe the hope portrayed in this passage.

The Christian view of life after death, "life everlasting," as stated in the Apostles' Creed, is a world characterized by resurrection and eternal life.

READ 1 THESSALONIANS 4:13-14.

How should the promise of bodily resurrection and everlasting life make it possible for us to mourn and hope at the same time?

Confessing, "I believe in ... the resurrection of the body, and the life everlasting" is to place our hope in something very specific about our future and the future of all creation.

How does this confession challenge your fears and hopes about death?

How can the Christian belief in resurrection and eternal life encourage you to walk in greater obedience?

The Apostles' Creed ends on an incredibly positive note by proclaiming our common hope: resurrection and everlasting life. The eschatology of our culture is built on progress. The eschatology of Christianity is built on death and resurrection. Our hope isn't in human progress but in God's raising the dead.

Why do you think some people in our culture choose to hope in progress?

How is the Christian hope of resurrection better than the hope of progress?

Father in heaven, You're the Creator of all things, and You've seen fit to send Your Son to be born of a virgin, to die on my behalf, and to be buried for my sins. However, the grave could not hold Him. By Your Spirit He burst forth from the grave. He left death in the tomb. I give my Lord honor and praise as He intercedes for me at Your right hand. I know it's good for Him to be with You in heaven and it's good that He has poured His Spirit on me from on high. Yet I long for His return. I wait with great anticipation and hope because when He comes, He will make all things new, and death will be forever defeated. Your church awaits You, Lord Jesus. Come quickly. Amen.

DAY 2

One error we need to avoid is the lie that because we have hope for eternal life, this earthly life doesn't matter. Even worse, it's easy to fall for the lie that anything physical or temporary is bad and only spiritual things are good.

What's the danger of dismissing anything in this world as insignificant?

Gnosticism was a heresy that plagued the early church. One of the main teachings of gnosticism was that all physical matter is evil, while all spiritual and immaterial things are good. Therefore, the gnostic view of life was that death would free people from the physical evil they couldn't escape. Gnostics taught that after death, humans left their earthly bodies behind and enjoyed only a spiritual presence with God.

In contrast, Scripture clearly teaches a bodily resurrection. After death, our bodies will be resurrected and transformed for eternal life with God (see 1 Cor. 15:49; Phil. 3:20-21). Our hope doesn't lie in escape from this world but in the transformation of this world. For Christians, changed lives, bodily resurrection, and eternal life aren't secondary issues related to salvation but are in themselves the ultimate hope of salvation.

READ ROMANS 8:18-25.

What's the hope that saves believers? How did Paul instruct the Christian community to wait for it?

Describe in your own words what a world without futility, corruption, and bondage would be like. What characteristics might this kind of creation have?

READ REVELATION 21:1-8.

What are you most looking forward to in this future home with God?

In what ways is the picture of humanity's relationship with God in the new heaven and earth similar to the way God created everything in the beginning?

The new heaven and earth described in Revelation 21–22 remind us of what Jesus instructed His disciples to pray for in the Lord's Prayer: "Your kingdom come, your will be done, on earth as it is in heaven" (Matt. 6:10). Think carefully about Jesus' words. He didn't tell His disciples to curse or destroy the corrupt world. Rather, Jesus' disciples are to pray for God's kingdom to come and change the world.

Notice Jesus' words to His disciples about praying for the new kingdom. How is this admonition similar to the redemptive fact that Jesus rose from the dead and will one day raise all His children from the dead?

Father, I, along with all creation, am longing for the day when You'll make all things new. Even when it feels as if I'm surrounded by death and disease, I believe You, through the resurrection of Your Son, are already making all things new. Amen.

DAY 3

Hope is vital, but misplaced hope is catastrophic. Why? Because you'll do anything for what you believe to be your ultimate hope. If your family is your hope, you'll compromise or sacrifice anything for your family. If your hope is in success, you'll do anything to succeed. But if your hope is in Christ and eternal life with Him, then you'll do anything for your King. There's nothing in this world that can destroy you or take your hope away. It's what you hope for and what you hope in that drive the way you live your life.

This is our hope. We have a God—Father, Son, and Spirit—who made us, loves us, saved us, and will resurrect us when He makes all things new (see Rev. 21:5).

Paul wrote, "The last enemy to be destroyed is death" (1 Cor. 15:26). Jesus' resurrection is the firstfruits of His victory. Someday all believers will be raised from the dead to join Christ in His triumph over death—physically, bodily, and gloriously.

Let's look one last time at our theological grid to consider the implications of the awesome hope we have in a bodily resurrection and eternal life.

1. SYMMETRY

What are you putting undue hope in that can't deliver true satisfaction, meaning, joy, security, and other things you long for?

2. CLARITY

How does belief in a physical, bodily resurrection affect the way you view eternal life? How does it affect your view of this current life?

3. COMMUNITY

Everyone you meet is created by the same God who created you. They're eternal beings who need the grace of God through faith in Jesus Christ.

How does this fact change the way you relate to other people? How does it affect your patience? Your eagerness to forgive? Your desire to share the gospel? Your celebration in their joy? Your burden in their suffering?

4. COUNSEL

Because all souls are eternal and will exist forever, what will you do to intentionally focus on your spiritual health and growth in maturity?

"The resurrection of the body, and the life everlasting"—this phrase is the foundation of Christian hope, Christian courage, and the ordering of the Christian life.

Review the Apostles' Creed. Which doctrines do you now see as more important or applicable than you did before this study?

How would you summarize the importance of right Christian doctrine?

What would you tell someone who asked what you learned in this study?

Prayer

Thank God that you're blessed to join the generations of saints who have come before you, who live around the world today, and who will come behind you. Praise Him for His grace in Jesus and His power in the Spirit. Pray that He will help you value the truth of His Word and the blessing of His church. Worship God now in light of your sure hope of eternal life with Him and His people in the new heaven and new earth.

Leader Guide

Thank you for being willing to lead a group through an in-depth examination of the primary tenets of Christianity. If this is your first time leading a group, don't over-think it. You'll just need to spend time in each week's group and personal studies prior to gathering with your group. Be prepared to distribute Bible study books and to view each video session. For session 1 you'll want to familiarize group members with the format of the study, including the way the group session will be structured ("Start," "Watch," "Discuss") and the features of the Bible study book ("Family Discipleship," memorization, and three personal studies). In addition, use the following guides to help you prepare for the group sessions.

GROUP SESSION 1

This first session will introduce the study and the importance of belief. Reemphasize Matt's point from the video that the Apostles' Creed holds no authority in and of itself. Scripture alone is the authoritative Word of God for our lives and churches. The creed is, however, an accurate summary of Christian doctrine affirmed by generations of faithful Christians throughout history. The doctrines presented in the creed will serve as an outline for our study of God's Word.

NOTES

GROUP SESSION 2

Beginning this week, you'll start each group session by reviewing the previous week's study. This is an important time of accountability and encouragement. Evaluate the time you've allotted for the session and aim to manage that time well, ensuring time to start with review and to discuss the teaching after the video.

This week introduces the first Person of the triune Godhead and three titles defining His character: Father, Almighty, and Creator.

NOTES

GROUP SESSION 3

At this point group members should start getting comfortable with the routine and with reciting the Apostles' Creed aloud together. Don't skip this part of the group session. As Matt said in the video session 1, the recitation of the creed aloud is an act of unity among all believers around the world and throughout history. It's also a statement of allegiance to our King and of nonconformity to this world.

This session introduces Jesus, the second Person of the Trinity, using three titles to define His character: Christ, Son, and Lord.

NOTES

GROUP SESSION 4

Weeks 4–8 continue to describe the person and work of Jesus. This week also introduces the third Person of the Trinity: the Holy Spirit. Much of the time will be spent on the Holy Spirit. However, remind group members that the Holy Spirit will be the exclusive focus of week 9.

You may want to be familiar with and even have access to a copy of your church's statement of faith about the Holy Spirit. It would be wise to have your statement of faith handy as your group discusses the various doctrines each week.

It's important to note that this week isn't ultimately about Mary. You may need to redirect the conversation if it gets sidetracked. The emphasis in the creed and in the Bible is on the activity of God in the incarnation of Jesus, not on why He chose Mary as Jesus' mother. However, Mary provides a beautiful picture of responding to God in faith, even in confusing or challenging circumstances.

NOTES

GROUP SESSION 5

The mention of Pontius Pilate is more significant than it may seem in a casual reading or recitation. Emphasize that the inclusion of Pilate affirms the historicity of these events as facts. They aren't merely religious beliefs; they're a part of world history under the direction of a political leader. The virgin birth is also a historical fact, although Mary wasn't a public figure.

The emphasis in this session is on the physical reality and spiritual significance of Jesus' death. While the brutality of His suffering demonstrates the wickedness of humanity and the severity of sin, don't allow the discussion to fixate on this point.

NOTES

GROUP SESSION 6

This session includes the most controversial phrase in the creed: "He descended into hell." The phrase isn't always included in the creed, depending on the particular church, denomination, or tradition. Matt chose to include it, approaching the subject as a means of emphasizing the totality of Jesus' experience in atoning for sin in death.

Be clear that hell is a reality, though little time is given to this point in the session. The focus of the teaching and discussion is on the fact that Jesus took on the fullness of our punishment in God's judgment of our sin before rising in victory over sin and death through the resurrection. The resurrection will be addressed again in the final week, but it's important to note that this was a physical resurrection.

NOTES

GROUP SESSION 7

The midway point is a good time to evaluate how the learning process is going. You may want to ask group members how they are doing with their personal studies, family discipleship, and memorization of the creed.

This session is one of victory and celebration after the previous weeks of suffering, death, and the grave. Much as the descent to hell highlighted the fullness of Jesus' death, His ascension to heaven highlights the fullness of His resurrected life. The emphasis in this discussion should be on the authority of Christ and on His ongoing power and presence by His Spirit.

NOTES

GROUP SESSION 8

Be prepared to keep this week's discussion focused on two points: Jesus will return, and He will judge everyone. It's likely that certain people in the group will want to discuss various eschatological views; some may even feel strongly that a particular eschatology is correct. Perhaps you enjoy these discussions. However, the emphasis of this session and of the creed isn't on how and when Jesus' return may happen. The point is simply that it will happen and that it will mean judgment. You may wish to provide a disclaimer or be ready, if the point comes up, to communicate that while the discussion is interesting and important, out of respect for time, the group needs to focus on the doctrinal points highlighted in this session.

NOTES

GROUP SESSION 9

This week's topic is another point of interest and strong opinion for many people. Again, you may want to be familiar with your church's statement of beliefs about the Holy Spirit. Time doesn't allow for an exhaustive study on the Spirit. This session will only be able to scratch the surface.

Just as you've approached the other doctrines in the Apostles' Creed, come prepared to answer questions or to direct people to resources, including church leaders, related to the topic. Avoid speculation or pressure to provide an answer. A major historical purpose of creeds was to articulate orthodox beliefs and refute heretical teachings that crept into the church, especially in regard to the Trinity.

NOTES

GROUP SESSION 10

If you haven't already done so, decide what you'll study after you finish week 12 of *The Apostles' Creed.* This session focuses on the importance of the church, so it's a great time to be sure everyone is committed to what you'll experience next. Scripture commands us not to give up regularly gathering together as a community of believers (see Heb. 10:25).

The terms *holy catholic, communion,* and *saints* may distract some group members at first. Be sure people understand that *catholic* means "global" or "universal," referring to the entire church—Christians around the world and throughout history. This term doesn't mean the Roman Catholic Church as opposed to evangelical churches. Likewise, *saints* refers to all Christians. We're made holy through Christ. Finally, communion isn't the ordinance of the Lord's Supper but rather the simple act of gathering in meaningful relationships as a community of faith. In the creed "holy catholic church" and "the communion of saints" are essentially synonymous.

NOTES

GROUP SESSION 11

At this point in the study, even if you were a new group, some level of trust and comfort should be established. This session deals with the forgiveness of sin and provides a natural opportunity to be honest with one another about salvation in Jesus Christ. Be prepared to lead a time of prayer for your group.

NOTES

GROUP SESSION 12

In this final session be sure to leave plenty of time to reflect on and review the entire 12-week study. This is an important part of processing and applying what everyone has learned. Discussion of what has been most meaningful to people is often a rich time of encouragement and honesty. Pay attention to what people say, because their comments will give you great insight into their need for further spiritual growth or into their readiness to take next steps in leadership. Communicate plans for when and where you'll meet next and what you'll study.

NOTES

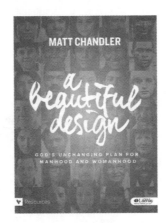